BETTY FEEZOR
A Life That Mattered

Betty Feezor
A Life That Mattered

Introduction by
TURNER COLE FEEZOR

Published by
TURNER COLE FEEZOR
Charlotte, N.C.
1978

BETTY FEEZOR: A Life That Mattered
Copyright © 1978 by Turner Feezor

Library of Congress Catalog Card No.

*Typography, Printing, and Binding by
Kingsport Press, Inc., Kingsport, Tenn.*

Dedication

To all of Betty's friends she knew, and to those she never met.

To the WBTV and WWBT people she loved, and who helped her to help others.

To *The Charlotte Observer* which helped her share her life with others.

Contents

PART I
BETTY FEEZOR'S AUTOBIOGRAPHY written by her after she discovered she had inoperable cancer of the brain and lung

Introduction by Turner Feezor	3
Early Childhood	5
First of Many Moves to Come	7
On to Little Rock	9
On to College	12
Completion of Education	12
God and My Career	14
Home Demonstration Agent — Blount County	16
Across the Mountains to Salisbury	17
Next to Greensboro	18
Television Career	20
Career vs. Children	23
Career and Homemaking Duties	25
Philosophy behind TV Show	26
Cookbooks	27
Funny Business	29
TV Mail	33
Commercials	33
Our Format	35
Color TV	37
Using Your Real Name	38
Questions Often Asked	39
Other Radio TV Shows	41
Professional Groups	41
Public Speaking	42
My Mother and Father	44
My Husband	48
Betty Cole Feezor	49

Contents

John Daniels Feezor	51
Robert Milton Feezor	52
Family Pets	53
Family Camping	55
Tour Guide	56
With God's Help	59
Human Relationships	60
Appreciation	61
News and Homemaking	63
Childhood Days	68
This I Believe	73
Cancer!	78
The Letters	79
The Last Chapter	86

PART II
BETTY'S DIARY   87

Introduction to Betty's Diary	89
Cancer Won't Beat Me	91
It's Awfully Important to Feel Needed, Trusted	95
One Day at a Time	98
Easter Was Very Special This Year	100
A Setback, and Time to Reflect	102
So Many Send Letters and Prayers	103
Luckily I've Found Fashionable Wigs	105
Slowing Down Brings New Pleasure to Life	107
Cobalt, Chemotherapy: Instruments for Healing	108
Feezor Diary Showed the Way	109
An Understanding Family Helps You Face Difficulty	110
The Greatest Healing of All Comes with Life After Death	111
I Have Memories I Can Call On	112
Be Positive About Life	114
Quiet Reigns, but It's No Time for Loneliness	115
I'm Beginning to Feel Like My Old Self Again	116
Instead of Worrying, I Count My Blessings	119
Children Cut the Apron Strings	121
The Doctors Brought Good News and Bad	122

Contents

Misfortunes Can Give Us a New Direction in Life	123
It Was a Busy Week . . . It's Nice to Slow Down	124
Many Dread the Thought of Cancer	125
How Would YOU Respond to Cancer?	127
After the Pain, There's Relief	128
Men and Women in Medicine Heed a Special Calling	129
Family Brings Appreciation	130
It Takes Time to Get Used to Slow Pace	131
Thankful for a Day Away, a Double Rainbow	133
Betty Feezor Prayer	134
Think First of the Sick When You Go Visiting	135
How Good it Is to Feel Good	137
Savoring the Beauty of Autumn	138
It's Time for Bringing the Things We Love Close By	139
My Pinch Hitters Come Through	141
Mom's Advice Stands the Test of Time	142
Time Adds a Touch of Humor to Past	144
Betty Feezor Grand Marshal of Carrousel	146
From Hospital Bed	146
Find Joy in Removing Routine from Your Daily Housekeeping	147
I Have Heard God Speak, and That's Why I Believe	148
Caring about Others Carries Its Own Reward	150
Back Home	152
Funeral Meditation for Betty Feezor	153

PART III
TRIBUTES TO BETTY   157

As Death Came, She Was Ready	159
Betty Was a Lady	162
Betty Feezor: Charlotte's Favorite Dish	163
A Lost Warmth — It Matters to Thousands Betty Feezor Was Here	166
Betty: A Neighbor to Thousands	169
Twentieth Anniversary	171

Contents

Tribute to Betty	173
A Memorial to Betty Feezor	176
Betty Feezor Fans Set up Scholarship	178
To the Times-News	180
Hers Was a Friendly Voice	181
Dear God: Re Betty Feezor	182

PART I

BETTY'S AUTOBIOGRAPHY

Introduction

I never fully realized how much my wife, Betty Feezor, meant to so many people until her death. Yes, she drew large crowds when she made public appearances. And she was always recognized wherever she traveled. And she received a lot of mail. But until her death no one knew just how deeply she had touched so many lives. Reading the cards and letters from friends and from people she had never met tells the story. "We lost a friend." . . . "A member of our family" . . . and "a teacher who made our everyday chores easier, who taught us to sew, to do needlepoint, to prepare better meals." — the list goes on.

To so many, her faith and character was such a comfort, an example to follow.

After reading all those cards and letters, I decided to share this book with you.

After Betty learned she had cancer and the doctor told us it was inoperable and that she had perhaps only 6 months to a year to live, we discussed what to do. Go to the mountains to live? That's something we had often talked about. Travel? That was something she liked to do. Just go home, rest and do nothing? Try another group of doctors at a different hospital? We could do whatever she thought best.

She decided she would beat the timetable the doctors gave her, making the best use of whatever amount of time she had left. To fight her battle, she would depend on Charlotte doctors for cobalt and chemotherapy treatments — and her faith in God.

As soon as her treatments gave her some relief, she started a large piece of needlepoint. She made ready to do some TV features. When Dave Lawrence, editor of the Charlotte Observer, asked her about doing some writing she accepted his offer immediately because this was something she could do on the "good days" and when she was not able to go out or do other things. She also decided to write this story of her life and beliefs.

These pages were written during her battle with cancer. The last chapter was completed just before her final visit to the hospital. This is part of her life dedicated to all those people she loved and whose lives she touched.

Turner C. Feezor

Early Childhood

Texarkana is one of those towns halfway within two states — Arkansas and Texas. When I was growing up, I thought those were the only two states in the United States. I was greatly disappointed when my father told me there were 46 others.

I was born on Feb. 17, 1925 in the Pine Street Hospital on the Texas side of Texarkana. Since my father was county agent for Miller County, Arkansas, we had to live on the Arkansas side of town.

Since I was very young when we lived in that apartment on County Avenue, I don't have too many memories of it. I do recall one terrifying experience though. A big dog knocked me down and stood over me in the front yard. To me, it looked like a lion or tiger. To this day, I have a fear of dogs. When I was a little older, before going to play with one of my friends, my mother would always call ahead to be sure that the dogs were tied up.

We had a tire swing too, under a tree in the front yard. I have several pictures of myself swinging happily in the summer breeze.

I loved playing dolls. Several other childhood pictures show me pushing one of my babies in a little doll buggy. My love of dolls continued for many years. In fact, my father worried about me still wanting a doll for Christmas when I was 12 years old.

My mother really believed in cleanliness. She must have bathed me and changed my clothes several times a day to be sure I met her standards of what a little girl should look like at that age. Once I asked her if it would be all right if I got dirty. I can't remember her answer.

When I was 5, we moved to a house. It seemed enormous then. In my child's eye I can still see the big rooms and front and back yards. Many years later, we visited my old home. I couldn't believe how really small it was. Of course, I was much smaller then, too.

My memories of that little house on Locust Street are pleasant. Within two blocks were many children who enjoyed playing together. We skated in the street, rode our bicycles and waded in the gutters after a rain. There must have been fewer cars in those days.

Of course, we had our "mean old neighbor" like other neighborhoods. Her children were grown. She could not tolerate any of us setting foot on her grass. Since she was mean to us, we were always thinking up mean tricks to pull on her. One Halloween night, in pouring rain, we were all ready to set a jack-o-lantern in front of her door and ring the bell. Just then, she opened the door. We were almost speechless. Despite all that rain, we feebly asked if we could look through her son's telescope in the backyard.

Directly across the street from our block was a vacant lot with what I remember as a big hole. Some boys evidently started digging the hole and had left it. We worked on it most every day. At times we used it as a hiding place from our mothers.

I went to Fairview Elementary School until the middle of the sixth grade. The school was seven blocks from our house. Until I could ride a bicycle my father would take me, or I would walk. He often came home for dinner in the middle of the day, so he would stop for me and bring me back one hour later in time for the bell.

I was never much of an athlete. While some of the other girls would play ball, I would play jacks or hopscotch. My fingernails were always kept short by the concrete sidewalks as I played jacks.

My father's office was in the Post Office which was situated on the county line. It served both states. He would walk down Texas steps to get to this Arkansas office. Perhaps you've seen the famous postcard of the man holding the reins of a mule in front of that building. The man was in one state and the mule in the other.

Then, my best friend was Maurine. We played dolls together every day — one day at my house and the next at hers. Often we played paper dolls. Each Sunday the colored comic section carried a paper doll with several outfits. We cut these out very carefully. To add to their wardrobes, we designed more clothes and added those to the paper wardrobes. We even cut out rooms from magazines. We would line up these like huge mansions for the paper dolls.

Maurine and I would play until it was time to go home, then walk halfway home with the other. One day we played until mid-afternoon, then stopped to clean out the storeroom on the back of our garage which we used as a playhouse. We swept it thoroughly, then took the little bit of trash to the vacant lot behind our house and burned it. When the trash was nearly through burning, we beat out the fire with our brooms and returned them to the playhouse. We had no idea there could be a spark left in one of the brooms. Later, when I got home our maid (who was keeping me that day while my parents were away) came screaming to tell me that the storage room had burned. A neighbor had called the fire department and had driven the car out. Foolishly, but luckily, my mother had left the keys in the car. I guess God looks out for us in ways that we never expect.

Ours was a divided home as far as religious denomination. My mother was a Baptist, and for many years she had played the organ at church. My father was a very staunch Presbyterian. Since they didn't attend the same church, they told me I could attend either.

I visited the Baptist Church with my mother. The preacher scared me. He shouted, and pounded with his fist. I chose to attend the much quieter Presbyterian Church with my father. I can still recall the calm I felt when I looked at the stained glass window where Jesus knelt to pray in the garden.

First of Many Moves to Come

In the middle of the sixth grade we moved to Fayetteville, the home of the University of Arkansas. I had been to Fayetteville many times to stay for a few weeks in the summers while my father completed his B.S. degree in agriculture.

It was always so much fun to be in Fayetteville. Mother and I would walk down the hill from the room where we stayed to the drugstore in the college shopping center. They had the best toast I had ever tasted. The cook brushed it with melted butter before placing it on the sandwich grill for browning. Each day, I had toast and chocolate milk for breakfast.

The school I went to was nothing like the one in Texarkana. It was only three blocks from the house we rented, but it was very old and foreboding. It was dark red brick with oiled floors and an odor that I would come to recognize often in years to come as I attended 4-H club meetings in country schools — dirty socks and tennis shoes. There is really no other odor quite like it, is there?

The principal, who was also my homeroom teacher, looked like Abraham Lincoln. He was tall and gaunt and rough looking without the tenderness of Mr. Lincoln's face. Soon after I came to this school, he and one of the tall sixth grade boys were having it out in the hall. The principal was trying to punish the student. I don't remember who won, but I remember my horror at seeing a student fighting with the principal.

Math has never been a strong subject for me. When I went to school in Fayetteville, the students already had started on algebra. I was afraid to tell my teacher or my father that I didn't understand. Instead I tried to memorize the formulas each day. I went to class fearful that the teacher might ask me to put one of the formulas on the board. I can't remember now what grade I made, but I learned that you really have to understand something before you can master it.

A few months later, I entered Junior high school. It was in a new building and I don't remember it as very much different from the junior high our children attended in Charlotte. And I remember my first boy-girl parties.

One of my fondest memories of Fayetteville is that of my handsome cousin who lived with us that year. I never had a brother or sister. Bobby was an engineering student who needed a place to stay. I was so proud to show him off to my friends. Over my father's strong objections, Bobby dropped out of school to join the regular Navy. Daddy reminded him that he would probably never complete his education. He did, though. After 20 years in the Navy, he went back to school and got his degree in engineering. He's now teaching in a college in Arizona.

During this time, my mother discovered she was a diabetic. She had to stay in the hospital for about a week learning to eat. It turned out to be a good thing for all of us because we all cut down on sugar. Before then, for instance, we had thought that to have really good grapefruit for breakfast, that we should cut it and load it with sugar the night before; that way, we thought, it would be sweet enough. Food tastes so much better, and it's better for us, with less sugar.

Mother always thought diabetes was the worst disease anyone could have. She never told anyone outside our family what was wrong. She could have done so much good for her friends and acquaintances if they could have seen how beautifully she followed her diet as a diabetic.

On to Little Rock

In June 1938, we moved again, this time to Little Rock. My father had been transferred. Little Rock, the capital city, is about the size of Charlotte. And there are other similarities. There are lots of roses in both cities; both towns are rather hilly in places, and have lots of friendly people.

My father had to travel quite a lot, and my mother was terribly afraid to stay on the first floor when he was away. Luckily, we found a lovely duplex located entirely on the second floor. The lower apartment was occupied by the owner and his wife and daughter. She was two years older than I, but we became very good friends. She already knew all the teenagers in the neighborhood. Very soon I had a whole group of new friends.

In the fall I entered Pulaski Heights Junior High. I was still pretty timid, but I made some very close friends who are still close today. We still write each other through a round-robin letter.

Six of us teenage girls spent a lot of time together. We went out to dinner together every Saturday night and to what we then called a "picture show." Most of us went to different colleges and ended up living in different states. All of us eventually married and lived far apart. We probably would have lost touch with each other if it had not been for the friend in Burlington, Vt., who wrote to each of us suggesting the round-robin.

We kept up with marriages, children. We shared problems in dealing with our families. We often enclosed pictures, so we could know each other through pictures.

During all the years we kept saying we should have a reunion. Finally the friend who lives in Little Rock invited us to come there on a day in April 1972. We all flew in. It was as if we hadn't been separated all those years since graduation in 1942. After three days and two nights of catching up on everything, we all went back home. It was one of the most pleasant experiences in my life.

First Attempt at Public Speaking

In the ninth grade, the most important thing that happened to me was finding that I could speak from a platform with ease. I took my only speech class that year. Our teacher made us spread out all over the auditorium and balcony. The speaker had to speak through the public address system so each class member could hear, and so we would learn to make eye contact with each individual.

That same year my best friend ran for student council president. She asked me to be her campaign manager which meant I would have to make a speech in her behalf. I had a stuttering problem and I was timid, but I decided to do it for her. I made the speech. My friend Shirley won the election.

My stuttering problem started in the first or second grade. I hated to stand in class and read aloud. I was always a poor reader, and other students would laugh at me when I mispronounced a word or just didn't know the word. Maybe this caused my hesitancy of speech.

The words I still have the most problem with start with "t" and "w." Others have bothered me at times. I had trouble saying, "This is Betty," when identifying myself on the telephone. Knowing that I would have a hard time assured that I would.

Two ways to help control stuttering are getting plenty of rest and speaking slowly. King George, the father of Queen Elizabeth II, stuttered. I can remember hearing him speak to his subjects very slowly. He was practicing this technique.

In junior high, I joined the drama club and was assigned a part. When I stood to read my lines, I had a terrible time getting the words out. I worried about the day when we would present the play before the class. Thank goodness, I got sick a day or so before the play was to be presented so someone else had to take the part.

On to Little Rock

Stuttering presented a real problem in doing commercials. As long as I was allowed to ad lib them in my own words, I was fine. If I had to read the commercial using someone else's words, I could be in trouble. If only I had sought professional help much earlier in life, I could have avoided lots of unnecessary heartache and embarrassment.

The other valuable lesson I learned in ninth grade was typing. My very strict teacher had a metronome at the front of her room and a stick in her hands with which she kept time on the desk or on our shoulders and even hands if we were not keeping time. The strictest teachers often are the ones we appreciate most in later years, and I can certainly say that for her.

Little Rock High School was the only white high in town at that time, so college preparatory courses were taught there as well as auto mechanics, beauty culture and many commercial courses. LRHS, as we so lovingly called it later, became Central High and this was where, in 1957, President Eisenhower called in the troops to maintain order after desegregation.

One of my most colorful high school teachers was Miss Middlebrooks. Some students called her Miss Centerstream, but all of us loved her. She taught college preparatory English, and did she ever teach us English?!

Knowing we would have lots of "pop" quizzes in college, she gave them to us in high school. We had to study all the time. This made my freshman English in college almost a repeat of the 12th grade.

I didn't study home economics in high school. I had taken the required courses in junior high, but my very wise father suggested I wait until college.

During my senior year, the United States entered World War II. When they announced the bombing of Pearl Harbor, I was at a sorority meeting. I remember going home and telling my parents about it. We looked it up on the map. The next day the principal called the student body into the auditorium to hear President Roosevelt declare war on Japan. We all wondered what war would be like.

In June 1942, our class graduated at night in the football stadium. The girls all wore long white dresses and carried a dozen red roses. The boys all wore dark suits. It was beautiful.

On to College

That fall, I entered Texas State College for Women. Several friends were going there and they had a good home economics department. So I went along, too. I really loved everything about Denton, Texas, and the school and all the girls. I wanted to graduate there.

Soon after Christmas, my parents called me to say that my father was being transferred to Washington, and that they would be moving soon. What bothered me most was that I wouldn't be able to go back to Texas State because of war-time travel restrictions. I felt that my whole world had fallen apart. One of my best friends comforted me by reminding me that everything happens for the best. This was one of the turning points of my life, leaving the Southwest and moving East as I did the next year.

Completion of Education

If you can remember travel during the Second World War, you know it was next to impossible for civilians to travel, particularly from such places as Texas to Washington. With this in mind we checked out the University of Tennessee. It was still far away, but not so far as Denton.

In those days colleges and universities were so anxious to have students that it was not at all hard to be accepted even just a few weeks in advance. I had no trouble getting into UT.

When the time came for me to leave Arlington, Va., where my parents were living in one of those temporary apartments, several of their friends came over to tell me goodby. One well meaning lady

On to College

started talking about all the terrible experiences she had heard about on pullman cars. I had to ride the train back to Knoxville. I remembered all she said as I undressed and tried to sleep in my upper berth. From then on, I was content to take the day coach and travel during the daylight hours between Knoxville and Arlington.

Housing conditions were very crowded in 1944 at many colleges and universities due to cadet corps. This meant doubling up in the rooms. Where there had been two to a room and four to a suite, there were now three to a room and six to a suite. Trying to get three girls' clothes in one closet was quite a feat.

The University of Tennessee had an outstanding home economics school then and it's still among the nation's top three. All my classes gave me the good basics that I would use the rest of my life.

As I look back at those college days which were so very different from what I had expected compared with my teenage memories of Fayetteville and the University of Arkansas, I still feel some resentment that my college days had to come when all the boys had gone into the armed forces and our school was so terribly overcrowded.

One course that most home ec students most looked forward to was a quarter in the "practice house." Each house was large enough for six or eight students plus the resident teacher.

We divided the duties — hostess, cook, housekeeper, and chief babysitter. The hostess planned the meals, ordered the groceries and was generally in charge for a week. The cook cooked according to the recipes supplied by the hostess. We had to serve liver once a week and eat it, too, because it was "good" for us. During my week as cook, I had to make a liver loaf using uncooked liver. I can still see and feel the ground liver. I have never eaten it since.

We had a baby from the welfare department in each "practice house." None of us knew much about looking after a baby. But we learned to love the baby, and it grew and prospered.

The head of all the "practice houses" was one of our least favorite teachers. Every day she inspected our house. Of course, we couldn't complain about her, but our baby sure could. Every time she walked through, our baby seemed to cry. We got a kick out of that.

Most students didn't look forward to the required food demonstration course where each student had to plan and prepare a recipe in front of an audience. It came easily to me. This along with my experience from speaking for my friend who was running for student council president in junior high started me toward a career in speaking before groups. I still use some techniques I learned in that course.

By taking a couple of correspondence courses between my junior and senior years, I finished my work in March 1946. Maybe that's why I could get a job as soon as I finished — I didn't have very much competition.

God and My Career

During my first 20 years, I asked God's help to decide in what directions to go, but He was doing more than I realized in preparing me for my life ahead.

In 1946 the main jobs open to graduate home economists were home demonstration agents (home economics agents as they are known now), home economics teacher, utility company home economist and a few jobs in business. Even though I had never lived on a farm and knew almost nothing about rural life except through my father's work as county agent, I was offered a job as home demonstration agent in Blount County, Tennessee. Maryville is the county seat and it's about 20 miles south of Knoxville.

Before accepting the job, I prayed for help in making my decision. Not long after, as I was walking down the steps of the S & W Cafeteria in Knoxville, God spoke to me. He told me that my first job should be the one in Maryville. After that there was no question in my mind as to the job I should take.

Barely 21 years old and looking so young, I was concerned about talking to mature women. One thing I really needed was stockings. In 1946 the only ones available were rayon. My parents came to pick me up after graduation and drive me back to Arlington. We stopped at each town along the way looking for any sort of acceptable stockings for me.

God and My Career

Before leaving for Maryville a week later, my father sat me down and gave some very good advice (and said he thought I would probably be back home in about two weeks; he probably knew that would make me even more determined to succeed). What he told me I follow even today. He said:

- Keep your mouth shut and your ears open. This will enable you to learn a lot without exposing your ignorance. (I don't always do this, but at times I do try.)
- Join a church as soon as you can. Here you'll meet some of the finest people of the town with beliefs like yours. (He assumed it would be a Presbyterian church. Sure enough, the First Presbyterian Church is the one that I joined.)
- Move to your new town and stay there. Don't go off every weekend to Knoxville to the university. This will help you to more quickly become a part of your new town. Also, don't talk about your hometown and how you did things there. This gets tiresome to others when you are trying to make new friends.
- Establish credit as soon as you can. Get a gasoline credit card so if you have to borrow money you'll have a better chance since you'll have paid your bills on time and be a good credit risk.
- In public speaking, don't try to be funny. You don't tell jokes very well, so don't try. Don't ever speak on a subject you're not familiar with.
- Choose friends other than those you'll work with. That way, you'll know people in different professions. And if you don't get along well with your co-workers, you can spend the rest of the time with friends of your own choosing.
- You'll represent the Tennessee Agricultural Service as well as the 4-H and Home Demonstration Clubs of Blount County. You as well as your car should never be seen in a place that you would not be proud of.

He probably gave me other ideas that day, but I particularly recall these 31 years later.

Home Demonstration Agent — Blount County

I asked my father why graduation from high school and college was called "commencement." He reminded me that in high school and in college you learn lots of facts with little opportunity to try them out. After all, everything seems to work right in class. It's only when you start putting the facts and formulas into practice that your education really begins. This was certainly true for me. I'm sure I learned more in my first year out than I did in four years of college.

There were tough lessons to learn in those early years in that rural county in east Tennessee. For instance, I knew very little about canning. I could get booklets on canning, but they never seemed to answer the questions when someone called. Thank goodness we had a secretary in that office for many years who knew many answers. I dreaded those times Delta was out of the office. Then, I'd have to answer the phone.

One new subject was "How to cull hens." I had never heard of culling hens, much less knowing "how". Of course, I wanted to change that month's topic, but Mr. Elrod, the wise old county agent, made me go through with it after he gave me lessons on culling the poor layers out of the flock.

Mr. Elrod taught me to pick up a chicken, how to hold one and how to pick the good layers from the poor ones.

When the time came to demonstrate at one lady's house, I spotted a chicken with many characteristics of a poor layer. I pointed it out, whereupon one woman then spoke up: "That's a rooster." I'll never forget how dumb I felt. I should have remembered what my father taught me — never talk about anything you're not well informed on.

One of my biggest problems in those early days of 1946 was not having a car. Those days, you had to put your name on a waiting list for a new one. After nine months, I was finally called and told my car was ready. I was so excited that I had to write out the check three times before I got it right. (My parents gave me that $1,275 car as a graduation present.)

That black car was a two-door Chevrolet without the features that would make it comfortable or attractive today. But it looked like a golden chariot to me. At last, I could drive myself to club meetings.

Until my car came, I totally depended on the two county agents to take me to meetings. As we drove along, they continued my education. They taught me about the breeds of cattle and hogs the types of grain and about other crops growing along the road. This was burley tobacco area, so I learned how it was grown and harvested.

Needless to say my "commencement" began in Maryville, Tenn. After three years in that beautiful county, I moved on to the other side of the mountains to North Carolina and Salisbury.

Across the Mountains to Salisbury

Salisbury was an older and larger community. Outside Salisbury, most people I came in contact with in the county were warm and gracious and welcoming. The much more reserved townspeople wanted to stand back and check me out before taking me into their hearts. After 18 months there I was just beginning to feel at home in the town of Salisbury as much as I did in the county of Rowan.

In Salisbury the Presbyterian church then was made up of older people. So I started attending the Baptist church, where I found younger people. I led a youth group on Sunday nights. The director of Christian education became a close friend. She encouraged me.

My apartment roommate was Mary Ellen. We started reading aloud to each other some inspirational things that each of us held dear. I had always had problems with reading aloud in front of others. So this helped me in my career as home demonstration agent as well as my television career to follow.

Later, I was offered a job as home demonstration agent in Guilford County (Greensboro). As with my other two jobs, I prayed and felt that it was God's will for me to go. I didn't know just what He had in store for me.

When I went for my interview, the county commissioners seemed most concerned about my age. I tried to look older, more mature, but I was still only 25. Finally, they decided to give me a chance.

Next to Greensboro

Greensboro turned out to be one of the nicest towns I had lived in.

In all the towns I lived in, there were young women who turned out to be life-long friends. Most of my high school friends and the friends I made in those towns where I worked are still in my address book. They are among those people who have taught me so much and have been loyal through the years.

In Maryville, I was the only home demonstration agent. In Salisbury I had one assistant. In Greensboro I had two assistants. There was a lot of turnover, since most assistants were right out of college. I helped find replacements for the jobs as they became available. One of these new agents turned out to be my future sister-in-law.

Even though I had pursued my career for five years, I really didn't want to become a "career girl." I wanted to get married. In Maryville I dated a very attractive young man with one of the loveliest families I had ever met. When we started getting more serious, I turned to God for His guidance.

After much prayer I didn't seem to get any answer. Finally, the answer came very clearly — he was not the one. I remember saying, "But God, remember I'm getting older. You don't really want me to be an old maid, do you?" I really thought He had made a mistake, but I later found out His plan is perfect and I should wait to marry the right one.

I had known Audrey Feezor Turner for some time, but not very well. Others in our office suggested I ask her if she might be interested in the opening we had. Before long she joined us in the Guilford County Extension Office.

Audrey and I became close friends. She kept telling me about her

Next to Greensboro

brother who traveled for a farm equipment company and came to Greensboro often. I was eager to meet someone new. Even before meeting him, I thought he might be a bit different from other young men I had met.

Audrey and Rucker had us to their house for dinner one evening not long after. I met Turner, and was immediately impressed with his maturity and solidness. He said little, but what he said had substance. He reminded me a lot of my father. Turner seemed to fit the image of a life-long partner I was looking for.

We became more interested in each other and talked of marriage. I prayed about marrying Turner. Shortly, God told me to go ahead.

We were married on Aug. 30, 1952 in Greensboro. Now, after more than 25 years of marriage, we both are convinced that this is one of the marriages made in Heaven.

Television Career

During my first 2½ years in Greensboro I not only met and married the man of my dreams, but I had my first experience with television. As the Guilford County home demonstration agent, I was often invited to the local TV station to present the projects of club members and to appear on panels. While some others seemed nervous, I felt at ease. In fact, I looked forward to when I would be on camera.

Gaines Kelly managed WFMY in those days. He wanted to start a homemaking show with me as the hostess, but since Turner and I were moving to Charlotte at the end of 1952, I had to give up that thought.

Turner and I moved to a two-bedroom apartment in one of Charlotte's two apartment complexes in 1953.

Now I had what I had always wanted — a loving husband and a place to look after. Turner traveled and had to be away two or three nights a week. It didn't take me long to get settled. I had much of the day with not much to do. I worked on some needlepoint, bought some plants, and added some decorator touches to the apartment. I wanted to do more.

I taught a Girl Scout troop about Red Cross first aid. Meanwhile, we joined First Methodist since Turner was a Methodist. I still had hours to fill. My years as a very active home economist had made me used to being on the go.

Then, a few weeks later, I received a letter from WBTV telling me that Mr. Kelly from Greensboro had written about my ability in front of a television camera. WBTV wanted to talk to me about substituting on Carolina Cookery, the first cooking show on that station.

Susie McIntyre had done Carolina Cookery for a year without a vacation. I was invited to fill in for her for two weeks so she could take time off. I wasn't tested or auditioned. WBTV trusted me, and I trusted them.

The only work I had done in front of a television camera was to talk — not to demonstrate food preparation. For the next few days, I worked out 45-minute programs for two weeks — five per week. I also planned for the 10 different dresses that I would wear. Even then I realized that what you wear is almost as important as what you show how to make.

My first day was Easter Monday 1953. The only recipe I can remember preparing was a mustard sauce for leftover Easter ham. Anyway, I had enough material to fill the time; when our director gave me a "cut" cue, I was still going strong.

Each day of those two weeks the director came down from the control room to point out what I had done wrong. I talked much too fast . . . I didn't know which camera to look into . . . I didn't pronounce my words distinctly . . . the list went on. I was grateful for the criticism. How else was I to learn?

By the second week I was much better, but still had several "accidents." On one show I had prepared a congealed salad, but, hard as I tried, the mold just would not come off. I was sitting on a stool working with the salad when, suddenly, it let go. The salad landed in my lap just as the closing theme song was coming on.

After those two weeks, I went home eager to do more. It was fun teaching in a new way.

Less than a month later, WBTV asked if I would like to do my own show. They suggested a twice-a-week show about any homemaking subject other than cooking. There were no sponsors, so it would be sink-or-swim. If we picked up some sponsors, the show would be kept on the air. If not, it would be cancelled. Starting in June 1953, the Betty Feezor Show started with two days a week and soon spread to three days a week.

Career vs. Children

As much as I enjoyed my new career, it wasn't nearly as important as starting a family. When after nearly a year of marriage, Turner and I found we were to become parents, we were thrilled. The WBTV folks were not quite so thrilled because the show was beginning to sell and nobody knew what to do with a pregnant hostess. This was 1954 when attitudes (especially mine) were very different from those today. My upbringing and background just wouldn't permit me to wear maternity clothes in front of the television camera.

So a substitute did my show for the five weeks I was away for the birth of Betty Cole on April 25, 1954. Her name was my husband's choice — my first name and his middle name. Cole was the name of one of his grandmothers and Turner the name of the other. We were very pleased with our choice.

When one of our friends came to the hospital to see us she said, "Oh, you named her after (WBTV personality) Grady Cole," we knew we might be in for some questions in the time to come, and we were. For years after, people thought I was Grady Cole's daughter and we had named Betty Cole with him in mind. Once someone sent me a photo of Grady Cole with a note saying they thought I'd like to have another picture of my father.

Betty Cole was my TV show guest on her first birthday. Beforehand, someone asked me what I'd do if she cried. Sure enough, she did. I guess we just made the best of it, since it was all live.

Our second child, John, was born Jan. 24, 1956.

In April 1956, Mrs. McIntyre decided to give up her show. Now I could talk about cooking, too.

With two children at home now, I realized I needed fulltime help.

Here again, God led me. I called and called on employment service but the line just stayed busy. So, I went to the agency and told the manager the sort of person I was looking for. Donella Mitchell was sitting there. The manager said she and I should get along very well together. It was love at first sight for us both.

Donella has not only helped raise our children and keep our house in good order, but has taught all of us ever so much. I've learned to be more organized just watching how she schedules her day's work. She's taught me it's better to go on with your work even though you may not feel so good that day. I would say, "Donella, you should have stayed at home today." And she would reply, "I won't feel any worse here than I would at home."

When Donella came to work with us, we were living in the duplex we had built with my parents. She had her hands full keeping the house clean and chasing after two small children, even though I was there much of the time myself to help. As the years rolled by, my mother required more help. She had several broken bones and other sicknesses, and Donella was right there to provide the help that she needed. When Mother could no longer drive, Donella drove for her. Mother continued to play organ for a local funeral home for many years, so Donella would drive her there and back. She bought Mother's groceries and did her banking for her. She would take Mother visiting. She became just as good a friend to Mother's friends as to ours.

In addition, Donella has always been a devoted wife and mother. She has a daughter and son just a month older than our Bob. She nursed her husband through a long illness and has brought up her son to be a fine young man. She is an outstanding Christian lady.

Career and Homemaking Duties

I was brought up to believe a woman's place is in the home. Even though my career was exciting and fulfilling, I tried to develop work habits to allow me to be at home as long as possible in the morning and come home as soon as possible after the show was finished. Even though I had lots of "homework" for my show I could fit that in with what I wanted to do for my family. When our children became school age, I worked out car pools to take them to activities. In fact when they were old enough to stay in school all day, they didn't even realize that I worked.

A TV homemaking show brought lots of mail. Even though WBTV handled the recipe requests, lots of personal letters had to be answered. I brought those letters home each day, wrote out answers and took them back the next day. We tried to make sure every letter was answered.

Some people would ask me to plan a party for them, send all of the necessary recipes plus ideas for games and tell them how to decorate. Naturally, this was impossible. We developed a form letter to say that I read all the mail and tried to work the questions and suggestions into the Betty Feezor Show.

Philosophy behind TV Show

God was with me all along, allowing me to go into the same type of homes by way of television that I had gone into so many times for club meetings. When I went into a home via TV, I could imagine just what that home looked like.

Knowing what kind of people were watching led me to offer information that was short and simple. Those watching seemed to appreciate recipes and other ideas that didn't require them to go to the store and buy special ingredients. Most of us would rather know how to remodel last year's dress than see expensive new ones modeled, dresses way beyond our means.

It just made sense to be timely. When my boys came in muddy in the spring, I figured most mothers had the same problem. In May, I usually started Bible school projects to give teachers time to see if they could use them in June or July. In spring, I concentrated on bridal fashions and how to make your own wedding veil.

It didn't take me long to learn to realize most people preferred a good basic pound cake or meat loaf recipe to a long detailed gourmet recipe. The sort of recipes Julia Child would use are fine for a more leisurely night-time audience, but they don't fit into a noontime format when there is no captive audience. At 1 P.M. viewers get up to answer the phone or door, or go to change the baby or all sorts of other interruptions.

When I used a recipe from a viewer, which was very often, I always tried to credit her. This brought me closer to the viewers.

From the beginning, I realized I'm not perfect and shouldn't pretend to be. The television camera really cuts you to the core in honesty. If you make a mistake and try to cover it up, it's very evident to those watching. If you expect people to trust you, be honest with them.

If I tried a certain sewing technique in making a garment, and wasn't pleased with it, I always confessed that I had tried something that didn't work too well. Then I went on to suggest alternatives that might work better.

Since I did so much sewing on my show, I wore clothes I made to show they didn't fall apart. For a long time, I didn't even have a ready-made dress in my closet.

When you teach in front of a TV camera, you tend to think of the audience listening together in an auditorium or stadium. Then you remember that viewers are listening alone or in small groups so you talk to them individually. I would think of the camera as my neighbor and talk to it as if I were visiting next door. I tried to use the same conversational tone as I did at home.

My early TV features displayed a rather stern face and attitude from me. But I soon loosened up and learned to smile more. Those half-hour smiles might be the only personal ones of the day for those who live alone.

At first I talked much too fast. People wrote that they could not keep up with me. I tried hard but kept returning to my original pace. I really don't know if I slowed down through the years or just educated my viewers to listen faster, but there were fewer complaints in later years.

Cookbooks

After I had been doing the Betty Feezor Show for a couple of years, viewers started asking for my cookbook. Turner and I started thinking this might be a good project for us and for my career.

We knew nothing about publishing. WBTV said I could promote the book on TV and even helped line up a publisher for us.

Meanwhile, I spent every extra moment gathering all my recipes and putting them into an acceptable book form. A local artist designed the cover.

In October 1957, the book was ready. We chose October because

we understood the biggest number of books are sold before Christmas. I told my viewers about "Betty Feezor's Best." Hereto-fore, when I had offered a recipe I had instant response. But it was different when I was asking $3 plus 30 cents for postage and handling. We got very few orders. We had put our own money into the book. I was sorry about not getting our money back, but I felt even worse because so few wanted the book. (Of course, it soon caught on and has been a best-seller since.)

Betty Feezor's Best was followed in 1964 by Carolina Recipes and in 1974, by Volume II of Carolina Recipes. When Volume II was published, we let Volume I lapse, thinking people would prefer the newer book. This hasn't proved to be the case. We got so many inquiries about the older book that we had it reprinted just as it was. Together, the two make a rather complete collection of recipes.

We've always taken care of the business of the cookbooks at home. They're stored in our basement and shipped out from there. This gave the children the chance to learn something about a family business and help with the bookkeeping and packaging.

John started at an early age in helping with the books. A nine-cent stamp would mail a book back in 1959. Turner bought them by the sheet and kept them in a special drawer. One day, we found John had pasted a 100-stamp sheet of them on our bedroom wall. He had done such a good job that we couldn't get many of them off. So we took a $9 loss.

Funny Business

When you do television live, as The Betty Feezor Show was for the first 16 years, nothing is done over again. In the beginning I wanted to correct errors of the day before. My director wisely counseled that I should just forget about it and try not to make that mistake again. Most of those watching didn't notice; calling attention to it would make it much more obvious. Over the years, though, I did correct any glaring errors.

Remembering my father's advice that I shouldn't tell jokes or otherwise be funny, the Betty Feezor Show was always completely professional. We joked before and after the show, but during that half-hour there was no funny business.

Incidents that seemed so serious then are funny as I look back.

For instance, when John Feezor was about 4 years old his father built a little car from an old lawn mower for him. The motor made that little car travel all of 4 or 5 miles per hour. John always wore his straw hat; seeing him in the car made a real cute picture. We decided to take the car to the TV station and let John drive the car on the show.

Betty Cole went along, too. When the time came for the car feature, John drove the car around. Then, he was to pick up his sister and give her a once-around ride. When she got on behind him, her skirt fell in front of a wheel. I stepped forward to pick up her skirt. John was ready to start and he did — knocking me flat down on the ground. I don't know exactly how I got up, but I did, in a lady-like way I hope.

If our children had done something special that I thought others would enjoy seeing, I would invite them to come. John was in kindergarten and had made a placemat using two pieces of wax paper with a fall leaf pressed between. Thinking this would be helpful to kindergarten and Sunday School teachers, I invited John to be on my show to demonstrate it "live."

He did a beautiful job with the placemat. I was so proud. Leading into my next commercial and getting him out of the studio, I offered him one of the frozen apple rolls that I was getting ready to advertise. He took one look at the plate and said, "I don't like those." I was horrified and responded, "Yes you do, John; you know you do." And he said, with a child's honesty, "No, I don't."

Everyone in the studio and control room just roared. I wanted to go through the floor. I *knew* we had lost a longtime sponsor.

The story has a happy ending. The sponsor thanked me for the commercial. How else can you call so much attention to a product! Viewers would go to their stores and ask for those frozen apple rolls that Betty Feezor's little boy didn't like.

John's brother Bob made his share, too, of the memorable mistakes on television. For many years I would have all three children on with me a day or so before Christmas. John and Betty Cole were never too eager but Bob was always ready to perform at any minute. On one of these pre-Christmas shows, Bob was demonstrating spray painting. I had told him that it is a good idea to spray into a box to avoid getting paint all over the surrounding area. Instead of letting him explain as fully as he wanted to, I interrupted to explain more fully. In turn, he interrupted me, noting, "Now, as I was saying . . ." He really put me in my place that day.

Another time, Bob was to cut cookies for Christmas. We had made the dough up and rolled it out before the show. He started cutting and just wouldn't stop. While I completed other features in the kitchen, Bob could be seen in the background still cutting cookies.

Betty Cole never had any interest in performing in front of the camera. Finally she and John were excused from what had become an annual chore to them. Bob still continued to come each year on his birthday, Dec. 23. He still looks forward to the Boy's Town Auction each year when he can perform in front of the camera as auctioneer.

Another live incident involved blenders. I had three on my demonstration table, all with glass containers. A cameraman was helping me move a tray and bring in another. During the switch, a container fell and broke. I thought I felt something funny running down my leg, but I couldn't stop and investigate. About 10 minutes later when I finished, I looked down to see a small pool of blood. It's a good thing the cut didn't happen at the top of the show — *and* that the cut wasn't too serious.

And there was another near tragedy. I was putting the beaters in the mixer, not realizing the mixer control was turned on. A cameraman plugged the mixer into the power while I had my left hand in the beaters. I still have scars on my left hand.

One day I made a cake. After the feature was finished, the cake was put on the floor. As the camera was moved a floor crewman stepped right in the middle of the cake. Thankfully, I didn't need that cake any more that day.

When Richard Nixon was running for vice president, Mrs. Nixon visited Charlotte. I asked her what she would be fixing for Mr. Nixon's dinner if they were at home that night. She went on to describe his favorite meatloaf. To my horror, when I got back to the studio I found someone had forgotten to turn on the sound so we had a silent film.

An annual Betty Feezor Show event around Christmas was a visit by the children from the Orthopedic Hospital in Gastonia. Each year, we gave plastic toys to each boy and girl. Once we got our dates mixed, and they arrived a week before we were expecting them. That called for some last-minute changes.

One visitor I remember especially was Mrs. Charles Cannon of Concord. The widow of the textile magnate, she was an invalid confined to her wheelchair for the last few years of her life. She spent a lot of time watching TV and seemed to like my show especially. She would have her cook take down many of my recipes and buy my sponsor's products.

Once one of her nurses wrote asking if Mrs. Cannon could visit my show. Naturally, we were very glad to have her. Her chauffeur drove right up to the back door. Her nurse and maid got her out of the car and into the studio before we knew what was happening. Mrs. Cannon seemed to enjoy every minute.

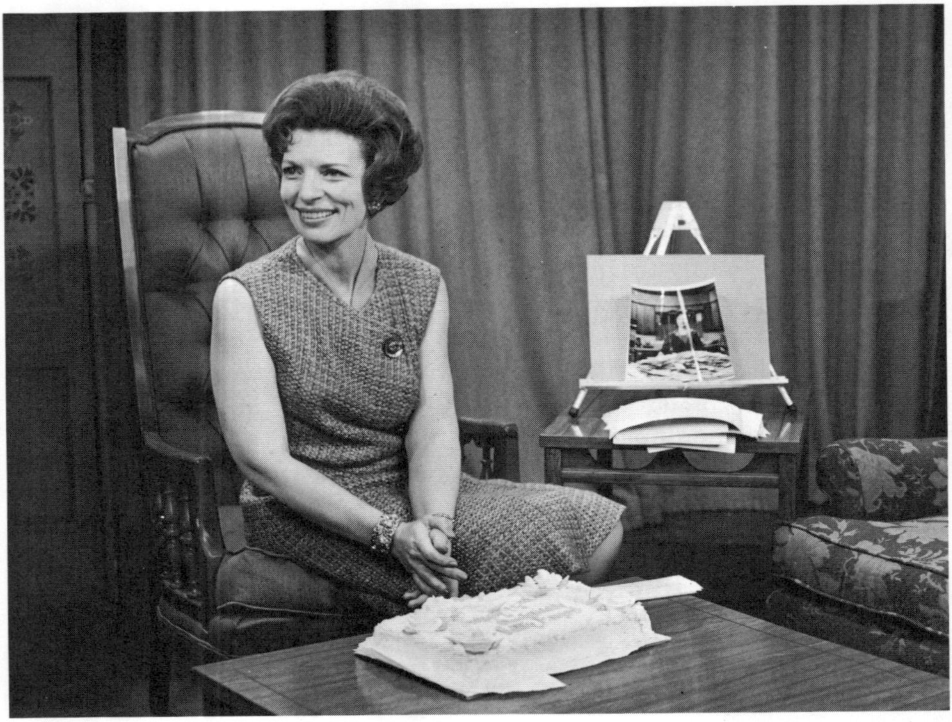

HAPPY 20TH
BETTY FEEZOR
WBTV
CHANNEL 3

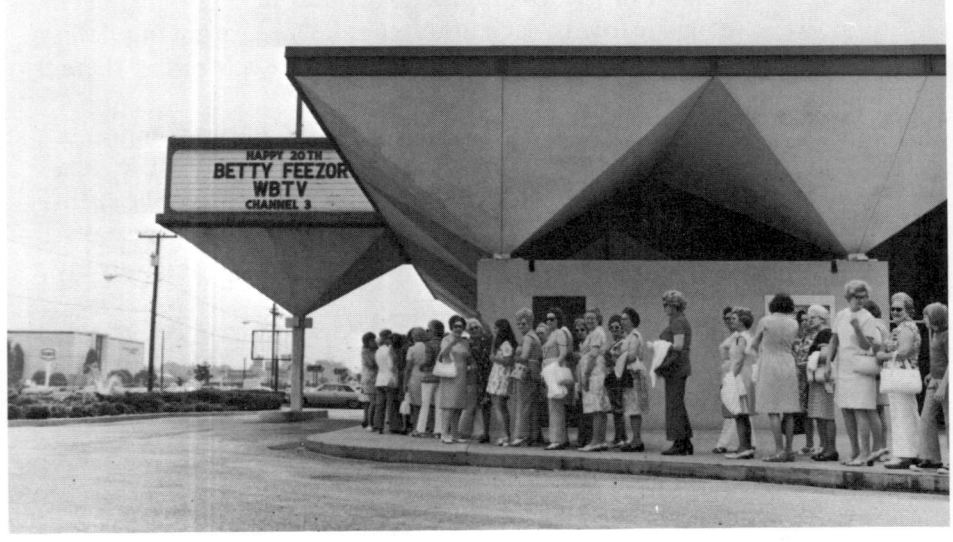

TV Mail

Mail is a very important part of a TV show. That's a good way to measure viewer interest. We averaged about 5,000 pieces a week. Most were requests for recipes. Some special contests and promotions would bring as many as 15,000 in just one day.

Over the years, I was always surprised there were so few critical letters. When I did get them, I very carefully answered them.

One unusual letter came from a teenager who had read that a movie star did not wear any underclothes. She thought lines would show in her outer clothing if she did. She thought I looked so nice in my clothes and wondered if I wore underclothes. I wrote back very quickly to explain the importance of being fully dressed from the skin out.

Another letter that stands out in my mind came from a man asking me to help find his wife. I wasn't able to.

Often mail was written in pencil on tablet paper. The grammar wasn't always perfect, the spelling was incorrect, but the meaning was sincere. This helped me realize who was watching the show.

For several years we invited women's groups to appear on the show. They would arrive in time to have lunch in WBTV's cafeteria, tour the building and take their seats on one side of the studio to watch and participate in the show. I introduced them with a little chit-chat about their club. We did this on Fridays, with a long waiting list of groups wanting to come.

Commercials

Doing commercials was one of the hardest things that I had to learn. When I worked for Agriculture Extension, I couldn't say any product was better than another.

Television was completely opposite. I had to try to sell a product

by name brand, giving the good points of that product alone and make people want to buy it.

Usually, TV scripts are written out, and we're supposed to read or memorize the script. I could neither read nor memorize very well, so I would just put the sponsor's main points into my own words. I'd tire of the same words day after day, and I felt the viewers had the same opinion.

Most commercials were written by New Yorkers who seemed to think everyone lived in their part of the country and spoke like they do. I found it much more believable to put the thought in "Southern English," so our viewers could understand better.

Lots of "pitch men" did commercials in the '50s when The Betty Feezor Show originated. This might be fine at certain times of the night, but a mid-day audience would better believe a soft-sell commercial . . . sort of as if I were talking to my backyard neighbor.

The FCC wasn't as strict in those days about how long commercials ran so it was easy to time the commercial with the feature material. One viewer told me she didn't even realize my show had commercials. It worked well. At one time, we had a waiting list of about 20 sponsers.

When you advertise a product in a live commercial, you are really endorsing the product. You associate your name with the product in a very close way. I've always felt it absolutely necessary to really believe in the product. I always used the product at home before I advertised it on TV. I wanted to be sure that I did not talk a person into buying something that I did not feel was a worthy product. Before any of our salesmen sold an account for me to advertise, he checked with me to see if I agreed to have my name associated with it. I did turn down several advertisers over the years. Several different discount and low cost ready-to-wear stores wanted me to do their commercials for them, but I felt I wouldn't do them any good, and I didn't think the association would do me any good at all.

If one advertiser ends his ad campaign, another sponsor must take his place even though it is a competitive one. This is a very touchy problem. Our policy required at least two weeks between advertising one product and switching to another. If I had been associated with a commercial for a long period of time, I required even longer.

The one that upset my viewers most was switching sewing machine sponsors several years ago. I had advertised one brand for many years with a very personal endorsement and used that machine often for sewing features. When we switched, I found I liked the new machine much better so I felt I could advertise it in good conscience.

That one sponsor switch brought me more criticism than anything else ever on The Betty Feezor Show. I knew I would never switch again from any other longtime sponsor.

Our Format

For 23 years, we relied on the same basic format. But we would keep the audience guessing, by doing different things on different days. Instead of telling the viewers I would cook on Monday, sew on Tuesday etc., our schedule was much more flexible.

We started out by telling the audience what would be included in the next half-hour. Four features were used, each one a different subject. Cooking was always included since everyone must cook most every day. Often one continuing feature was used for the whole week; for instance, making a dress.

The Betty Freezor Show was live for the first 16 years. I didn't realize how much more time-consuming it was for me to go to WBTV about 11:30, do the show live and get home about 2 o'clock. This broke my day right down the middle. If I went shopping in the morning, I had to stop in time to get to the station by 11:30 or noon, I didn't get to try to do many errands on the way home because I wanted to be there when my children got home from school. And I wouldn't go to luncheons or meetings at noon.

The Betty Feezor Kitchen is in Studio One. Beginning in 1960, a live news show — first called The Noon Report, then changed to the Scene at Noon — was done live from Studio Two. To save studio space, The Noon News show was moved to Studio One. This meant I had to prepare for my live show while another live show was on the air in the same studio. I had to wait for a film commercial to make any noise such as getting out pots and pans. It worked a hardship on both shows.

In 1969 our assistant program director suggested my show be taped earlier in the morning, then played at 1 P.M. We taped the show as if it were live. If I made a mistake, we just went on. We wanted the show to continue as much like before as possible. In future years, after the tape was played here, it was sent to our sister station in Richmond to be played there a week later.

Jefferson Pilot Corp. bought the Richmond television station in 1970. It was called WWBT to fit with WBT and WBTV in Charlotte. Since the Betty Feezor Show had been so successful in Charlotte, that station decided to use my show up there. Virginia homemakers are not so different from North and South Carolina and Tennessee homemakers. To me, it was like adding some more family members to my audience. Now I had to think about 30,000 more viewers — and that they were in a different location.

During the years our show was aired in Richmond I was invited to make many appearances. Several times, I went up to tape a five-day series. On my first visit, they surprised me with a new kitchen

Color TV

in the corner of a studio. It's almost like the one at WBTV.

Two or three times over the years, a Richmond appearance of mine would coincide with a farm equipment convention for Turner. It was fun to have our careers require us to be in another town at the same time.

On one such occasion, we were having dinner at our hotel. I was expecting a call from WWBT so we were listening carefully to intercom announcements should the call come during dinner. The waiter paged "Betty Furness." Thinking he had Feezor and Furness confused, Turner asked him. "Do you mean Betty Feezor?" He replied, "Yes, I guess so." I went to the phone, expecting a familiar voice from WWBT. Instead an operator asked for Betty Furness. It seems she was in the same restaurant and had a speaking engagement in Richmond the next day. I apologized for intercepting her call, and found her to be the charming lady she has always appeared to be on TV.

Color TV

WBTV has always been very progressive. Led by Charles Crutchfield, we've been among the first to try new things and to get new equipment. We bought one of the very first color cameras and the first color tape recorders sold to an individual TV station. The camera was bought in 1956 and the tape machine shortly after. Way back then, they decided my show would be in color every Thursday. We only had one color camera which meant the only variety in shots could come in the zoom lens instead of switching between cameras. My movements had to be much slower, so the camera could keep up with me.

Our show was put on tape about 10:30 and played back at its regular time of 1 o'clock. This was a record for local TV. It was the very first time that a show had been taped in color and played back in regular schedule on a local level. It was a day long remembered. So few people owned color sets in those days and there was so little network color programming that before long we put our color camera away. We tied a ribbon around that camera and decorated it with a flower and buried it in a closet at WBTV. Several years later we got into color telecasting with two new color cameras. Telecasting in color required nearly twice as much light as working in black and white. More lights were added to Studio One. Those years we worked in black and white, I could say these were green maraschino cherries when they were really red and no one knew the difference. Now we had to be very careful about the colors of food and other items.

Changing to color also meant I could no longer wear the black and white clothes I wore so often. Black absorbs so much of the color surrounding it. White tends to reflect on the surrounding colors. Medium pastels work in TV color. Suddenly, I found myself needing more color clothes so I got busy making them.

Using Your Real Name

Exposure through television means instant recognition when you appear in public. It's very flattering to know people watch you on TV and recognize you in public, but it can present problems, too.

One example is grocery shopping. Invariably, someone wants to know how much flour I used in that cake last week, or she'll need some help with a weeping meringue. More than once, I've gotten home without everything on my list because someone stopped me. Of course, when you're not recognized anymore it means you're no longer effective. Had I realized when I first went to WBTV that I'd be there 23 years instead of just two weeks, I would have used my maiden name or chosen a stage name.

Turner quite often is recognized as Betty Feezor's husband. Many men wouldn't like this but Turner has always been sure enough of his own identity not to be bothered.

Feezor is an unusual name, and we used to be the only Feezors in town, the only Feezors in the phone book. This brought lots of calls from viewers, often at the wrong times. And there were crank phone calls from children and, occasionally upsetting calls from strange men. Eventually, we decided to get an unlisted phone number.

Turner's cousin, a doctor, moved to Charlotte. Naturally, Dr. Feezor's name had to be listed in the phone book. So many people called asking for me that Mrs. Feezor called me one day to ask if I could announce on my show that I am not the doctor's wife. Using our family name on TV brought some problems to our children. Fellow students were always asking them if their mother is Betty Feezor. Our daughter had a good comeback. When asked, "Is Betty Feezor your mother?" she would say, "No, I'm her daughter." Our children enjoyed my career in many ways, but when they were growing up they got a little tired of the name association.

Questions Often Asked

When people learn you're in TV one of the first questions they ask is about the food. They want to know what happened to the food when the show is over. The answer is, of course, that the crew eats it. We always had a policy that if you did not work the show, you did not get to eat the food.

A lot of people think the lights must be very hot and blinding. The lights *are* bright, but your eyes adjust. In fact, when the lights are not on, it's hard to see in the studio even though the ceiling studio lights are on. Our studios have such good climate conditions that on most days the temperature is very comfortable.

People would ask about preparation time for the Betty Feezor Show. Turner would say it took about 24 hours for each show. It did take a lot of time, but I was able to work that time in and around taking care of my family. It never seemed time-consuming.

Many viewers asked how large my staff was. There were only the secretaries who took care of the mail. Once I found someone to help me with my sewing. She was an excellent seamstress, but it took too much time to bring the pattern and fabric to her and to follow up on the phone with details on making the garment. Eventually, it was easier just to do it myself. Then too, I could help viewers more with the construction if I made the garment myself.

The viewers have been very helpful. They sent not only recipes but also lots of craft and better-method features. A viewer often would send step-by-step illustrations for a better way to do such things as putting on a pocket. And companies sent ideas and prop kits that helped supply me with up-to-date material. The question of clothes also arose frequently. Appearing before the camera five days a week means you need lots of clothes. Most of my clothes were made as sewing features, and I ended up with more than I could use myself.

It wasn't uncommon for a viewer to write asking that I send clothes. I did send some to a couple of people who wrote, only to find their neighbors started writing, too. From then on, I suggested they find local help.

Viewers wrote in to ask if I were ever scared. No. . . . I never really was. In fact, I felt as easy in front of a live camera as in front of a live audience.

The only time I remember being tense was when I had a guest that I was not sure of. Then, too, having too many guests would sometimes make me feel a little nervous, or if we ran late in getting ready when the show was live. If I had enough time to familiarize myself and my guests with that day's topics, I was completely at ease.

Some people have a knack for operating in front of a camera, and others don't. I've seen experienced public speakers "freeze" in front of the camera. I find great warmth from the presence of live people as you speak or perform that you don't get in a TV studio with only four cameramen and a floor manager, none of whom are especially interested in what you are saying.

Other Radio TV Shows

Even though I don't have a trained voice, I was invited to work in radio from time to time. A Betty Feezor Show ran on WBT-FM for several years. I taped five 5-minute shows at one sitting, working in commercials as I went along. All went fine except for the time I had finished talking for 30 minutes straight, then was told by the producer that the tape wasn't loaded correctly and that I would have to do it all over again. That FM show lasted until the station switched to a full music format.

In 1954, Alan Newcomb, the beloved announcer and weatherman, and I did a show called "Doing It Yourself." It was one of the first local shows with a national sponsor.

In the early 1970's, I did a five-minute show called "Ask Betty." Then there was "Betty in the Morning," a five-minute bit that the program people hoped would help to keep viewer interest up during the early lineup. All these shows served their purpose at the time, but were short-lived compared with The Betty Feezor Show.

I grew up with radio. I well remember sitting in our living room and listening to all the night-time shows. One summer my mother and father and I spent six weeks in Minneapolis while my father worked on his graduate degree at the University of Minnesota. While he attended classes, Mother and I would listen to one soap opera right after another. Back then, I didn't have the foggiest idea that my voice would ever be heard on radio.

Professional Groups

I did feel it important to associate with a few professional groups. When Turner and I first moved to Charlotte, I joined the American Association of University Women. That gave me a chance to meet women of different ages and professional backgrounds. Later I had to drop my membership as my duties became heavier, but I still treasure the friendships from those days.

The professional group most closely associated with the TV industry is American Women in Radio and Television. It was so nice to get to know other people across the state who do the same sort of thing I do. In the early days, there were only four or five other women who worked in front of the camera as I did, but we exchanged ideas and problems to good advantage.

In later years the organization seemed to change, emphasizing the advertising end of TV. And so I dropped my active participation.

But the group nearest my heart has always been the Home Economics Association. I joined as soon as I finished college, and have been a member since.

In my years on TV, I continued to call myself a home economist. I felt this would encourage lots of girls watching to become home economists, too. Perhaps it would bring a certain prestige to my profession. I really believe it did.

Soon after I gave up The Betty Feezor Show in 1977, the Southwestern region of the North Carolina Home Economics Association set up a Betty Feezor Scholarship. It will help worthy home economics students attend a college or university in North or South Carolina to major in home economics. The fund is growing steadily. It's one of my greatest honors.

Over the years, there were many awards. For instance, the 1958 Junior Woman's Club Homemaking Award, the 1959 First Lady in Food in North Carolina, the 1967 and '69 TV-Radio Mirror for Outstanding Programming in Broadcasting, Outstanding Career Women in Broadcasting in 1973. My greatest honor came from the opportunity to teach people through television for so many years.

Public Speaking

I got so many invitations for speaking engagements. I tried to accept as many educational and religious invitations as my schedule allowed. And, of course, I didn't accept a speaker's fee for these. If an honorarium was given, it was donated to a charity.

Public Speaking

Whether I spoke to a school group, or a commercial group, I always tried to bring God's name into the speech. People expect fulltime religious workers to talk about God, but didn't expect it from me. Sometimes that makes more of an impact.

Speaking to a live audience is so much warmer than talking to a TV camera. Looking into people's faces, hearing their laughter and watching for signs of acceptance of you as a speaker — all mean so much. Usually I drove to where I made speeches. Once, I flew in a single-engine plane with one of our salesmen and a pilot. I didn't like the idea very much, but it did seem better than driving 100 miles there, then back at night. The idea of one engine concerned me, but the idea of the pilot not knowing exactly where the airport was scared me. As we flew near where I was to speak, the pilot and salesman conferred several times on the location of the field. It was a very small airfield. Finally, we landed. It rained the entire time we were there. We boarded the plane for our flight back to Charlotte. The rain continued to come down, and lightning danced all around us. I was so scared. We made it home, but I vowed never to fly in a one-engine plane again, especially at night.

The absolute worst ride that I ever took for the sake of TV was in a covered wagon behind two one-ton-each oxen. Our son, Bob, was seated next to me. Both of us were dressed in early-American clothes. Since we knew nothing about driving a covered wagon, someone else was hidden beside us to guide the oxen. The terrain was terribly bumpy. I was really terrified. Later, when I watched the show on TV I wondered how I ever had the nerve to participate. Bob thought it was great.

Through the years I've talked with lots of public speakers who have studied much more than I. We have much the same techniques, though. Most importantly, you need to talk to individuals in the audience. Don't look only at those people in the front rows. Look into individual faces throughout the auditorium. It's natural to look most often at those folks who are nodding or smiling in agreement as you speak.

Thirty minutes is plenty long for most speeches. Look for signs of whether the audience is still with you. When they start looking around, at their watches, even shaking them to see if they have stopped running, you might as well stop talking; conclude your speech even though you haven't finished all the points you planned to make — you've already lost your audience.

Some people read speeches very effectively. If the speaker must read the speech, it's so much more effective to look up at the audience as often as possible.

I've always found I would get closer to my audience if I kept the remarks light and with some relationship to what they were familiar with. Even the most serious subject can be handled with some levity in it. But, avoid a lot of jokes. The speeches I enjoyed making most were those made as a lay speaker in churches and before Extension Homemakers clubs.

Speaking in church allows you to stand high in the pulpit, close to the choir. When you sing you feel like you have a beautiful voice, too. And the physical height of being in the pulpit gives you a feeling of authority; commands respect.

Once Donella Mitchell invited me to speak at her church. I had never attended an 11 o'clock service with an all-black congregation. I'll never forget it.

All the hymns were sung a little faster than in my church. Even the Apostle's Creed was recited much faster. I could hardly keep up. But the music was the most special. The combination of the organ and a piano with the lovely voices sent chills through me. When my time came to speak, I was a little nervous. Never have I had the feeling of being quite so well accepted. Every person in the congregation later stopped to speak to me and thank me for coming. The experience was exhilarating.

My Mother and Father

When you try to be a homemaker and wife and do a daily TV show plus a few public appearances, a lot of fine balancing is involved. I thought of all activities as a balance scale. On one side I placed my family. On the other side I placed all the other activities I enjoyed. When I found my family side getting a little light compared

My Mother and Father

to the other side, I cut out some activities. I just didn't feel right letting some things I liked to do interfere with the more important family situation. I probably passed up some pretty exciting things but it gave me peace of mind that I wasn't slighting my family.

My family has always meant a lot to me — starting with my mother and father. Both grew up in Arkansas — my father in the southeast part, my mother in northeast Arkansas.

My father was the youngest of four children. My grandfather not only ran the farm, but did some surveying as well. He died while my father was in his second year at the University of Arkansas, so Daddy dropped out to return home and manage the farm for his mother. He joined the army in World War I and saw action in Europe. He became a captain in the infantry.

He was the very first "county agent" in Batesville, Ark. He moved into a boarding house near my mother's home. He used to tell me that when she knew he would be going by, she would start sweeping the sidewalk so she could see him. They were married in a small wedding in Batesville. On April 20, 1922, soon after, they moved to Texarkana where my father became Miller County's first county agent. My mother was a lovely lady — and I emphasize the *lady*. Her father died of diabetes when she was only 5. Her mother went back to live with her father and serve as hostess in a large house with lots of company. She was raised to have the polish and manners befitting a young lady of those days.

Even though mother wasn't brought up to do much work around the house, she learned how quickly when she had her own. I remember her as a fastidious housekeeper. She didn't like people to drop in unexpectedly for fear everything wouldn't be in place.

My father, John Buford Daniels Jr., was the most influential person in my life. He didn't tell me what I had to do, but he let it be known what he expected of me until I was married. Then, he became a very good father-in-law. He seldom offered advice unless asked.

My father was quiet, but when he said something it was worth listening to. He was very methodical and planned ahead in everything he did, not only in his jobs but in his daily living as well. He was enormously respected in every town in which we lived. I was always proud of him.

One thing he held most important was my education. Since I was an only child, it was very important to him that I be able to look after myself. His plan was that I go to college and major in home economics since that field would guarantee that I could get a good job. After graduation from college he wanted me to work for two years to prove to myself and to him that I could support myself. Then I could come home and he would look after me. Of course, after two years I wouldn't have given up my job to become dependent on him again. I'm sure he must have known this.

When Mother and Father were living in Washington in 1944, he had a heart attack and was hospitalized for two months. He was in a veteran's hospital with several other men in the same room and he also had lots of company from his office. Some even brought papers and reports for him to read and sign. All this was pressuring him, but he said nothing. The day before he was to go home, he had a second heart attack. The rest of his life was different. He learned you can't hold all your emotions inside of you.

My father retired with a disability in 1954. He and Mother moved to Charlotte to be near me and their first grandchild. We decided to build a duplex together. He was able to enjoy a yard after living in apartments for 15 years. He had planted roses and had made a hotbed for annuals. He went out every day to watch the house being built.

Then, he had another heart attack. He lived only two days. We had a hard time understanding how he could have his retirement planned, his new life all set, then die only six weeks before moving into our new house. Time helped us all to understand. His planning had prepared a comfortable home for my mother to be close to us, yet retain her independence.

Mother and Father had never been wealthy people, but they were always comfortable. Mother taught herself to sew. She made clothes for herself and me, and even for my doll. With all her creativity, she could use one pattern to make many different styles. And she did lots of embroidery and crocheting. Best of all she made, from string, two beautiful bedspreads that I still use in my home today. She never cared for cooking. Luckily most of her married life someone did that for her. Later when they moved to Washington my Father would beg her not to have company at home because she got so upset about wanting to have everything "just right." Usu-

My Mother and Father

Betty and Her Mother

ally, they took friends out to avoid her feelings of inadequacy.

When Father retired and they moved to Charlotte, she happily cooked for the two of them. After my father's death, she cooked only for herself. I was always proud of her for eating properly because it's so hard to cook meat and vegetables for one. As a diabetic, she knew how necessary it was to eat what was on her diet.

One day, she got tired of cooking for herself. She announced to Bob, "I am just going to eat dinner out every night from now on." She did for years. She and a friend frequented the neighborhood cafeteria every night. If the friend couldn't go, she would take John or Bob or Betty Cole with her.

We had a decision to make when we built our new house in 1969. Mother was very content to stay in the duplex we had built together, but we were running out of room on our side. Finally, we decided to build an apartment in our new house. All of us realized we needed our privacy and independence, and that we would remain much better friends if we didn't actually live together.

She could shut her door for complete privacy and lock it at night as she always did. Inside her part of the house we built a living room, bedroom, combination kitchen and eating area and bath. She was so proud of it and so happy that we wanted her to be with us instead of in a retirement home.

Mother developed a respiratory problem in October 1973. She was in and out of the hospital many times before she died on April 19, 1974. My father had died on April 20, 1955 (their wedding anniversary). Mother was buried April 20. I've always liked to think they had the happiest wedding anniversary of all when they were united in Heaven.

My Husband

The second most influential man in my life has been my husband, Turner Cole Feezor. One thing that attracted me to him were the same fine qualities that I admired in my father. Ours was not exactly love at first sight, but it soon grew into a lasting love.

Turner didn't have exactly the "easy life" I had in growing up. One of five children, he grew up in Davidson County. He worked on his father's farm as a boy. From 15 on he was pretty much on his own financially. His parents, both teachers, had the fine qualities that parents should have in raising a close, loving family. Like so many others who grew up without much money, he has often said that they didn't realize they were underprivileged. Turner had several jobs that provided the income and experience he needed. He often has told our children about working at a department store for only a few cents an hour for long hours. When he had saved enough money for an education he went to Brevard, N.C., and completed junior college.

He didn't get to the last two years of college and regretted it terribly when he started looking for a job. There were several jobs he really wanted, but was turned down because he didn't have a college degree. But it has all worked out well for him. In 1948 Turner became a salesman for the Ford tractor distributor in Charlotte. He is a natural-born soft-pitch salesman. In fact, I've learned a lot about doing commercials from watching him sell. Patience is one quality I admire most in my husband. When our children were young, his endless supply of patience in working and playing with them astounded me. I remember his spending hours teaching the children to ride their bicycles. I remember, too, the swings and slides and toys that he so lovingly made for them. The neighbor children most often played in our yard, because we had such unusual things to play with. Faithfulness is another quality that stood out to me. He not only has loved the children and me, but he always remembered his family with frequent visits and help when they needed it. When we were first married, I thought anyone so considerate of his parents would be as considerate of me. And he has been.

Turner can look so much farther down the road than I, so he has guided me through some difficult times. He has always seemed proud of what I have tried to accomplish. He's always bringing me suggestions of what might interest my viewers. He reminds me where the people live who watch television. As we ride along, he will point out the small houses with TV antennas on top and notes there are many more of these homes than affluent ones.

I admire his faithfulness to his church. He has been a Methodist all his life. He taught Sunday School in his home church and still supports that church in many ways. In our own church, he has been active in his Sunday School class as well as on the Finance Committee. He was in charge of raising the church budget two years in a row. I'm proud of him just as I was of my parents.

Betty Cole Feezor

After we were married in 1952, I was anxious to start a family. We were so excited when we found out we were expecting our first baby. Betty Cole was born April 25, 1954. Some of the qualities I remember from her first days reflect her personality today. She was born a week early, and it always seems to me that she was anxious to get here and get going. She has been going ever since.

Betty Cole was a very inquisitive child. She didn't require much sleep so that meant constant vigilance on my part. Through her curiosity, she broke many pretty things at both her grandmother's house and ours so we always thought it was better to leave our home as is and not put everything away. Children must learn what they can play with and what they can't.

Betty Cole loved to draw and write on the walls with crayons. I first saw her math ability by the neatness and formula-like quality of her drawings. Once I came home from the station to find her standing in her bed drawing the marks she could far as she could reach above and to the side of her baby bed.

Because playing dolls had been so important a part of my life, I just naturally thought Betty Cole would like dolls. She didn't and I felt she was "cheating" me out of a second time around of playing dolls. But she did like stuffed animals and those ugly little plastic beatnik dolls so popular in those days. She and a friend very elaborately named the dolls. In fact, everything she played had a well organized and mathematical sense.

She was an excellent student from the first. As soon as she got home from school, she'd make her brother sit down while she taught him everything she had learned. He patiently let her tell him.

When she was in the ninth grade, her teacher asked the students to start thinking what they would do when they finished school. She chose math and computer science and stuck with her plan through high school and college. This saved her time and our money because she didn't switch majors. In addition to her scholastic achievements, she was very active in school government and other activities. We could not have drawn blueprints for a daughter we would have been prouder of.

She chose Duke University and took a double major of math and computer science and graduated cum laude in 1976.

After graduation, she went to work for a small but growing company, Social Systems in Chapel Hill. That company sells its service to some of the largest firms in the U.S. Her job requires lots of travel, and that's exciting in your first real job.

John Daniels Feezor

John Daniels Feezor was born Jan. 24, 1956, 10 days later than his doctor predicted. His tardiness in arriving has set the pattern for his life. He takes things much easier than his sister and younger brother. He'll probably live a much better paced and longer life.

Unlike his sister, John has never been an A student. He loves the outdoors, has always enjoyed fishing and, in recent years, hunting has meant a lot to him.

John's always had so many friends. While his sister and brother had a few friends at a time, John always had a yard full. John has always been our quietest child. He would be content to sit in his high chair playing with a toy while I got dinner ready. He would swing in the backyard or ride on his rocking horse for hours. To this day, like his father, he doesn't talk a lot. He is very comfortable to be around.

Deer hunting is his passion. He hunts some of his great uncle's property in Davidson County. After two years of hunting, he finally got his first deer. It's mounted in our den.

His cousins taught him to clean the deer as well as hunt it. And his aunt has taught him to cook it. He takes great pride in having some friends over for deer steaks or chops cooked on the outdoor grill.

John has attended North Carolina State University for three years. During the summer he works for a construction crew building houses. Being outdoors even on a 100 degree or 32 degree day seems to suit him better than sitting in a classroom. We parents think our children should fit a certain mold and perform a certain way; it's hard to let go and let each child decide for himself.

Robert Milton Feezor

Robert Milton Feezor was born Dec. 23, 1959 two weeks early. I mention how early or late each child was born because that seems to be reflected in their personalities. Bob seemed so anxious to get here and has been running ever since.

Unlike brother John, Bob always has been more interested in inside activity. He is interested in music, performing, anything that puts him in front of the public. These qualities must have come from his grandmother and me.

Bob takes up one activity at a time and explores it completely before going on to another. His first passion was listening to Mary Poppins records. He would dress up like a Mary Poppins character and sit for a long time just quietly listening.

As he got a little older, he fell in love with Holiday Inns. He spent lots of time making Holiday Inn signs and even put some in our front yard despite his grandmother's concern that someone actually would stop for a room. Turner often took Bob with him on business trips so that he could stay at the Holiday Inn. Bob also loved a small, not very modern but clean motel in Sparta in northwestern North Carolina. He loved to go there with his daddy to spend the night and eat pancakes for breakfast while his father went about his business with his farm-equipment dealer in that town. Bob would stay at the motel helping the owner change the beds and clean the motel. Often when Turner stayed there by himself, he'd call us so Bob could talk to the owner. They became very close friends. Bob's next passion was the presidents. He memorized many facts about each one that really paid off later in school. After he mastered that next came the states and their capitals. Then it was aquariums followed by a CB radio. Each activity consumed him for a while.

When he was 10 or so, he became interested in the piano. My mother had a piano in her living room, and Bob would have her show him how to put his fingers on the keys. He didn't want to study piano because it was easier to pick out the tune by ear. He took

Family Pets

lessons for a few months, long enough to learn the notes. Since, he has become quite accomplished in reading music and adding his own embellishments.

In high school, Bob has been active in drama, the choir and student government. He hopes to major in radio, TV and drama in college. His father and I hope he will get a good liberal arts foundation as well.

Family Pets

With three children we were bound to have pets around the house, too. The first was a black cat that appeared at our door. Betty Cole and John watched after her for a while, but later I had to feed her each day. Then there came a time when the cat was going to have kittens. I was pregnant with Bob, and our house was being painted so I decided to give the cat away. When Turner found out, he said, "I didn't give you away just because you are pregnant." I felt sort of ashamed for not consulting more with the family.

Then there were the dogs. The first was Prince, part German shepherd and part-collie. He was beautiful. We had to keep him in our large fenced yard since he would threaten to bite people.

Beside our duplex was an apartment with a long paved driveway between our house and that apartment. Once, it had been snowing for several days and the children were using their sleds down the sloping driveway. Prince wanted so much to get out and play with them. When someone went through the gate and didn't fasten it securely, away he went. He ran to the front of the house just as a neighbor walked by wearing a face mask against the cold. Maybe the mask set him off, but Prince bit the neighbor in the leg. The dog pound people came out and checked him and told us to keep him locked up as we always did. We paid the medical bill and pants repair. We felt genuinely bad about what happened. Some months later, I saw our neighbor at a PTA meeting. Startled to see him, I asked about his leg and he said, "Here, do you want to see it?" Of course, I didn't, but he pulled up his trouser leg to reveal a scar. I couldn't think of a thing to say.

After Prince, we had Casear Feezor, (a beagle) and Duke (half St. Bernard and half Ilewyllen setter). Bob was helping to look after puppies which belonged to a neighbor. He was doing his yard-cutting job down the street. Caesar went along to keep him company. A truck came by, Caesar ran out in front of it and was killed. The driver helped bring Caesar home. With tears in his eyes, Bob buried Caesar. The gift of one of those puppies helped fill the void for Bob. Today, Duke barks a lot from his large fenced-in area behind our house. He's still quite a guard dog.

We've had several chickens in our family, too. One Easter the children got two chicks. They lived on and on. One was a rooster who would crow and chase Betty Cole and me every time we went into the backyard. Finally we convinced the boys it was time to get rid of him. We arranged with the Harris Teeter grocery store to buy the chickens. Receiving some cash eased the hurt. Another grown-up Easter chicken was taken by a WBTV cameraman to a farmer neighbor. Bob kept wanting to visit the chicken. I had to keep thinking up excuses not to go, fearing the chicken might have become a satisfying meal.

And there was an Easter duck who grew into a beautiful example of duckhood. He died of natural causes.

One day, John came home so excited. A friend had given him two gerbils. I wasn't so thrilled. A year later he gave them to a neighbor.

Then there was the turtle that kept escaping. We found him several weeks after his last escape, under a dresser and all dried out.

Our most unusual pet was a boa constrictor. It was in John's room in an old aquarium with heavy books atop. It ate a live mouse once every two weeks. When feeding time came, John's friends and Betty Cole's came to watch. The snake finally died, but I feel I'll have stars in my crown when I get to Heaven for allowing our son to keep a snake in his room.

Once, Bob decided he was going to be a chicken farmer and his father helped him buy two Rhode Island Reds. He wanted hens so they would have eggs to sell. Turner and Bob built a pen in our backyard. The first morning after they got them, Bob looked at the nest before he went off to school. When he came home from school, I don't know who was more excited at finding two eggs — Bob, his grandmother or me. I didn't understand why those two eggs were white and all the rest were brown. Many months later, Turner confessed he had put the first eggs in the nest so Bob wouldn't be disappointed. White eggs were the only color we had in our refrigerator.

Bob got a dozen eggs every week. He wouldn't let me have any of them. He preferred to sell them to his regular customers. He learned a lot from that experience. So did I — Rhode Island Reds lay only brown eggs.

Later on, Turner told Bob he was going to ask Santa Claus to bring him some bees for Christmas. One day I came home to find a very active hive of bees in my yard. Bob, the only chicken farmer in our neighborhood, was now the only boy in junior high with bees. And, as far as I know, I was the only mother ever to have to take a close look into the hive when they took the honey — at least the only one in our neighborhood.

Family Camping

We discovered family camping when the children were very young. I had never enjoyed 4-H Club camp when I was working, but family camping was fun. Turner wouldn't believe I would tough it out even one night, so we rented equipment for the first trip to Julian Price Park near Blowing Rock in the North Carolina mountains.

Betty Cole and John enjoyed bringing water and building a fire. Bob was less than 2, so Turner built a "house" for him next to our tent. Amazingly, he was content to stay in that area.

We had fun watching the children enjoy nature, and it was nice not to have the phone ring all the time. I was content with fewer dishes, fewer clothes, less clutter. And the children learned you can do things without flipping a switch for everything.

Next summer we bought a tent camper. Over the years, we went on numerous weekend trips as well as to such long-distance places as Key West and Texas. We often talk about our fun times together. Betty Cole and I don't think it is as exciting as it once was, but Turner and the boys still occasionally go to the beach to fish and stay in our camper.

I remember two nights camping out as the most uncomfortable. One was on the very top of Seven Devils Campground near Boone. It got so cold that Turner heated some rocks, wrapped them in towels and put them in our beds to keep us warm.

Another night at Grandfather Mountain it was raining and freezing cold. By the time we fixed our supper, the rain was coming down furiously. After supper, we drove to the top of the mountain and the temperature had dropped to 45 degrees. There was nothing to do but go back to our trailer and get in bed. We got very warm and told ghost stories, then fell off to sleep. The next thing I knew it was morning. I still remember the warm feeling of being so cozy in the bed, as well as the warm feeling of our family so safely secure.

One of our most exciting nights, especially for the children, was at Cades Cove, Tenn. We heard there were lots of bears in the campground so we weren't at all surprised to hear them later that night. Turner and the two older children went in the car to hunt for the bears. They found them enjoying leftover watermelon. Bob and I were alone in the trailer, I became a little uneasy. I was very glad to see the others return to protect us from the bears.

Tour Guide

In the summer of 1968 I became a tour guide, working with a travel agency and asking viewers if they would like to join me. We worked up a group of 27 of the very nicest people for a trip to Hawaii. I was a little uneasy about escorting a group of strangers on a trip like that but I figured that anyone who would be attracted to me would have the same habits as I do. It turned out to be a very congenial group. As soon as we landed, we saw the most beauti-

Tour Guide

ful rainbow. That brought us good luck for the rest of the time.

Betty Cole went with me that time. She was 14 then and she enjoyed all the sights and learning to water ski. To remind her of the trip when she got home, each day she wrote a letter to herself and sent it back. When we got home, she had a whole journal already written.

Our tour group got along so well that we planned a trip the next summer to Mexico. The nine women and one man on this trip found Mexico City fascinating. After several days, we flew to Acapulco for two days. John had planned to go, but changed his mind at the last minute. John's name was still on the list of returning passengers. An airline official came aboard to ask where John Feezor was. They wouldn't take my word for it that he hadn't come. Apparently they thought I planned to leave him down there. We went into the terminal to find everyone we needed to see was at lunch. Stacks of unfiled papers were on top of the filing cabinets. Our case looked hopeless. Finally after going through some unfiled lists atop the filing cabinet, we found the arrival list and, sure enough, John's name wasn't on it. It's a funny feeling to be in a strange country and feel powers-to-be aren't really interested in your welfare.

In 1970 many of our same group took a cruise through the Carribean. We sailed from Miami, stopping at several ports including St. Thomas. We all decided this is the last of the luxurious ways to travel. It was nice to unpack just once and use the cruise ship as a hotel. About half our group got sick, John (who did accompany me on this trip) and I did not.

In 1971 it was Bob's turn. Our trip was to Europe. So many wanted to go with us that we ended up with 44 people and a second tour guide. The trip was ill-fated from the very beginning. First, just half that number would have been much better. Our first stop in London was just fine but from there on, it was one mishap after another. When we got to Amsterdam we found no deposit had been made on the rooms; the hotel manager wouldn't let us in until some arrangements could be made. Half of us had to stay in another hotel.

The next morning, we were to leave for Germany. The bus from the other hotel was late in arriving at the airport, so some of us went on to Germany while the rest of us waited for the others in Holland.

I felt strange with my 10-year old son in one country and me in another.

After that, we thought everything else would be fine. That was not to be the case. We had been booked into a German hotel as a student group with several to a room and a bath down the hall. I was so upset by then that I placed a call to the travel agency and waited in the cold damp lobby for the return call. As a result, I got a terrible cold. We did enjoy our voyage down the Rhine, the nice clean beds and the good German food.

Our next stop was Switzerland. When our bus rounded the corner and we saw "Welcome, Betty Feezor Tour," our spirits were raised. We had a lovely hotel and delicious food and a magnificent trip across the Alps to Florence.

The bus almost didn't make it to our hotel in Florence. After a good dinner, we were ready to see some beautiful art the next day. We were awed by all the beauty of that city. In Venice, our bad luck returned when we discovered a hotel strike. The linens had been laid out, but we had to make our own beds and carry our own bags. It was worth the inconvenience to be able to see this decaying city, which is sinking a little each year.

Things were marvelous in Rome. Visiting the Vatican was a highlight of the trip. Then, we went on to Paris. Now, the trip was too much for Bob and me. We both got sick. A 10-year-old can go to bed, but the tour guide must go on no matter how she feels. After a couple of days I was completely ready to start home.

We boarded our 747 at Orly Field. Surely, nothing else could happen to us now. The food was American, the movie was Patton, so I settled back to enjoy the trip home. We had not been out of Paris more than 45 minutes when the pilot came on the loudspeaker and announced a bomb threat. He said we'd have to dump our fuel and head back. The attendants told us to prepare ourselves for an emergency landing. We had to leave our shoes and anything sharp on the plane.

In less than 45 seconds, we evacuated the plane and ran across the field to the terminal. Imagine the mass confusion of trying to call home to explain what had happened and trying to get all our possessions back and booked on another flight home. Word never did get through to our families about what happened. The information on the board in Charlotte just said "Cancelled." Our families had gone out to meet us and were very upset.

Finally we got to New York. A bus took us to LaGuardia to the plane that would take us to Durham and on to Charlotte. But when we got to Durham, there was one less seat than there were people. God must have been with us even through all our problems — they let me have the last seat. Only when I called Turner to tell him of the final arrival time did I break down and cry. The tour leader must be strong and not panic. By this time, all my strength and determination had been drained. When we finally landed, I swore I would never leave Charlotte again.

But less than a year later, WBTV asked me to escort a group to the Mediterranean. We went to Lisbon, Madrid, Athens and to Rome for Easter Sunday. While the first European trip was full of mishaps, the second was perfect — even the weather. Spending Easter Sunday at the Vatican was an experience I'll cherish the rest of my life.

Our last trip together was to the Pacific Northwest. It, too, was just about perfect. The scenery in Canada and San Francisco is hard to beat. Bob went on this trip and on his first train ride.

This trip turned out so well that I decided to put aside future trips. Members of our original group still continue to travel together. I just enjoy receiving the postcards from faraway places and remembering all the good times together.

With God's Help

One great decision we make with God's help is that of a spouse. After we've chosen, the wedding plans start. Often they're so elaborate or time-consuming that we forget the vows we've made in the ceremony. We promise God — not the minister or only each other — that we will live together for better or worse, for richer or poorer, in sickness or health, to love and cherish, till death us do part. I even promised to obey. Many young couples write their own vows these days with other commitments.

In Turner's and my case, I assumed that our marriage would be better, richer, with no sickness and plenty of love; that we would live happily ever after, never thinking of death at all. Perhaps if we periodically renewed our vows to each other, we would be able to "tough out" some of the rough spots in marriage. Perhaps one reason for so much separation and divorce today is not paying enough attention to the promises we made.

Human Relationships

Before marriage, we are the sons and daughters of our parents. Then with marriage our relationships change. Our Bible tells us we should leave our parents and cleave only to our husband or wife. Not that we should turn our backs on our parents, but we must realize the new relationship is now the most important.

Despite all the responsibilities of building a home, raising children and making a living, this basic relationship must always come first. It's hard to leave children with a relative or babysitter when they're little, but it's so important for the husband and wife to have some time to themselves. Some couples I know plan on one night a week to go out, even if it's only for a ride or an ice cream cone. We need time to talk and to reassure each other that we love each other.

Next on the list of relationships should be the children. When they are little it seems they should be the center of interest in the home — and sometimes they are. As they grow older, we should let them be more independent and not an excuse for our staying with them all the time. After all, when they're gone, we will be back to the primary relationship of husband and wife. Then, we need to be able to talk to each other and still have something in common. If the children are the center of our lives, we can lose the basic love of our spouses. Maybe this causes the breakup of so many marriages which have lasted two decades or more.

Then, the next important human relationships are mothers and

Appreciation

fathers and aunts and uncles and other relatives. We shouldn't forget any of these. Sometimes, we need to pay them first attention for a period of time. To keep safe the primary husband-wife relationship, we must learn a spouse's thoughts usually are more important than another family member's.

The husband and wife need to agree on how to divide duties. Ours has always been a "liberated" marriage even though I didn't realize it years ago. In the beginning, we agreed on who would do what. Turner is the president and treasurer of our family — I'm the vice president and corresponding secretary. It's worked all these years. Naturally, we discuss all the problems and decisions we need to make, but I like Turner to be the "boss" in our family, to make the final decisions. As I've heard so many people say, "You can't have two presidents in one company. The employees won't know who to follow." That's true of children. A strong father image leaves them with a more positive attitude toward family life.

Although lifestyles and marriage principles have changed greatly, it's still important that husband and wife agree on major things in the marriage. Just as important is presenting a united front to the children, reaching agreements beforehand instead of deciding in their presence.

Appreciation

No matter what's decided about who does what duty, that duty is done more easily if it's appreciated. Often, we are more courteous, more appreciative of others than of our own family. A "thank you" helps keep a happy home. When speaking to an audience of men and women, I've often asked the women how long it's been since their husbands came in and said, "Darling, you washed the windows today. They look so nice." The ladies usually laugh. Then I ask the men how long it has been since they thanked their wives for a nicely laundered shirt hanging in the closet, or socks washed and folded together in the drawer. This last example once brought this comment: "No one ever pairs my socks up. We just have a sock drawer for all of the males in the family. When you need socks, you just go to the drawer and find two that go together." I reminded him that someone first had to wash them and deliver them to the drawer.

I remember a story that illustrates the importance of expressing appreciation. A very wealthy lady lived in a large house on a hill. Behind her, in a much more humble home lived the gardener's wife. The rich lady was mostly interested in herself and what made her happy. The gardener's wife tried to help others first, often overlooking her own comfort.

When the rich lady died, she went to Heaven. St. Peter welcomed her and led her down beautiful streets. As they passed each big house, she thought surely that would be her heavenly home. But the houses got smaller and smaller until they were in a section of very modest homes. Here they stopped. The rich lady told St. Peter, "I couldn't possibly live here. I have always been used to much more than this." And St. Peter replied, "All we have to build with here in Heaven are the bricks in the form of good deeds that you send up from Earth. You have sent only enough to build this small home."

When the gardener's wife died, she, too, was met by St. Peter. He started their tour of Heaven in the section where the rich lady would spend the rest of eternity. The gardener's wife expected to stop at any of these houses, but they kept on going. Finally, they stopped in front of a magnificent home. She said, "But, St. Peter, I've never been used to anything so fine. I don't deserve this." And St. Peter replied, "All we have to build with are the bricks that you send up from Earth in the form of good deeds. You have sent enough to build this large home."

Now I don't believe we get to Heaven by doing as many good deeds as possible. That takes belief in Jesus Christ as the Son of God, but I also believe that when we believe in Christ we will want to do more things for others. So anytime that I do a good deed and receive no sign of appreciation, I just stop and think, "There went a brick."

Not only is expressing appreciation important to others in our families, it's very important to let them be individuals. If you have a large home, perhaps each child can have a room of his or her own. If not, try to set aside at least part of a room for privacy. Sharing is often learned in sharing a room.

It's difficult to accept members of our families as they are. We love them so much it's tempting to tell them what to do in all situations, so they'll be like we want them to be. Many little things that bother us about others really aren't important.

It's also hard not to compare one child with another. Grades, manners and accomplishments are just a few comparisons that we too often make. Our homes certainly would be monotonous if all our children were alike. We would do well to appreciate their differences and accept the fact that God made them as they are. If He can accept them, surely we can.

Trust is another important value. Let our children know that after we tell them the rules and demonstrate a good pattern of life, then we will trust them to follow through. This trust is demonstrated in the smallest ways. When John, our elder son, was just a very little boy, he awoke one winter night cold and maybe a little scared in his bedroom next to ours. He called out to his father who told him to come on and get in bed with us. Turner turned on the light which blinded John. I told him, "Just hold out your hand, and your father will show you where the bed is." John did just that, putting his faith in his father who proved trustworthy in helping him into bed with us.

Parents make a mistake in trying to present a perfect image to children. At a very early age, children should recognize that we, too, make mistakes. If we can admit to children that we made the same mistake once and thus we understand their feelings, we'll become much better friends in the long run. We've always told our children that the mistakes are less important than the way we recover.

News and Homemaking

Parenthood and homemaking mean many joys, but life can get very "daily." Washing the same dishes, chasing the same dust, and picking up and washing the same clothes gets a little monotonous.

News and Homemaking

The Feezors at Home.

The Feezors at Supper.

News and Homemaking

Many years ago I learned a valuable lesson from one of the first newswomen to work before a TV camera. Anything, she said, can become interesting if you make it "newsworthy." And this can mean household tasks, too.

Don't think of washing as a chore. Think of yourself as a textile chemist. Stand before your washing machine and look at all the laundry products in front of you. As a textile chemist, you can decide whether to use hot, warm or cold water. You also can decide on what type of detergent, water softener, bleach, etc. Now it's not a "chore." Laundry is something you can look forward to.

Knowing how much I really like to wash clothes, Bob came in one day with the dirtiest shirt I ever saw. I asked him why he had gotten his shirt so dirty and he replied, "I know how you like to get out spots and stains, Mom, so I thought I would make you happy this afternoon."

Use the same approach on sewing. Don't think of yourself as *just* a seamstress. Think of yourself as a dress designer. As you create a dress, imagine it as an original. No one will make the same mistakes that you make on yours.

Hate to cook? Think of yourself as a great chef. Learn to prepare one special meal that you can depend on every time. Even if the same people come for dinner often and even though you feed them the same thing, they'll look forward to it just as you look forward to going to a favorite restaurant for the same specialty. A friend of ours always has shrimp that we shell ourselves as we sit around her table. We always look forward to that special meal. And remember, even a frozen dinner tastes better if you place the contents on a china plate. Add an extra garnish. Your family may never know the difference.

Think of yourself as a safe and concerned chauffeur instead of just taking your turn at car pooling. When you work in the yard, imagine yourself as a landscape artist. Even taking the garbage out becomes more challenging if you're a "sanitary engineer," keeping your kitchen and family free of germs.

Hate to wash dishes? See how many steps you can save as you clear the table and stack the dishes. You can become an "efficiency consultant."

These techniques make life less "daily," and could change your ideas about the drudgery of homemaking. For me, it works on everything except cleaning house — especially running the vacuum cleaner. I still haven't found a way to make that fun.

Childhood Days

To make homemaking more exciting, we can change how we do things. As the expression goes, "Today is the first day of the rest of your life." Apply this to family life, too.

Ask your children what part of your house they like best. Their answers may surprise you. Our children told us their first place was the basement. We were surprised, but the children explained they could skate, build a spacecraft, have plays or bowl down there — and not have to clean up after each use. Surely, I thought, the children would like the living room best. That's the room I had worked the hardest on.

Their next favorite was the backyard. I know it didn't look half so nice as the front yard. With three children and assorted friends and a dog that ran all the time, that backyard did show a little wear. Again, the children explained that they could do a lot of fun things back there without having to be so careful about not messing it up.

Often, we inflict our ideas on our families. Some homes I've visited, the family members couldn't wear shoes in certain places, so the carpet wouldn't be marred. The husband couldn't smoke cigars in the living room. Chairs and sofas were covered when not in use. To me, the house belongs to all family members — not just the one who keeps it clean.

* * *

One night I asked our children what they liked about Daddy and me. Only silence . . . No one spoke up, and so I asked what they didn't like about us. John spoke up quickly and said, "Mom, I just wish you wouldn't scream at me so often." I wasn't aware that I screamed at him, but I guess I had screamed.

We decided on a truce. Even though our three children had

Childhood Days

separate bedrooms with just the right desk and lamp, John's favorite study place was the kitchen table. We agreed he would do his homework there while I cleaned up the kitchen. If he wouldn't "bug" me, I wouldn't scream at him. This was to continue until 8. At that hour, he asked for another hour. I readily agreed. John's bedtime was 9 in those days, so that would put him up to bedtime. About 8:30 he announced he was going to bed. Surprised, I asked him why he volunteered to go to bed a half-hour early. He replied, "I'm enjoying the peace and quiet so much I don't want to do anything to change it." I learned a lesson that night.

Our children have also taught me about nature and thoughtfulness. Most of what I remember this way came from our son, Bob. He's always been the most exuberant of our three.

Soon after we moved into our new home, he called me frantically to the carport. What, I wondered, was the matter. "Step outside, Mother," Bob said. "It's one of those you-can't-feel anything days. Just warm enough and cool enough that you can't feel the air." I've often thought of that every time we have a "just right" day.

Another time, we were staying at the beach in a travel trailer. That whole trailer was carpeted; I knew who would have to clean it up before we left. Each time somebody went in or out of the door, I knew more sand was being brought in for me to clean away. Bob insisted I go outside. I did so reluctantly. I'll always be grateful that I did. Bob showed me the sun was setting on the same level of the horizon as the moon was rising. I've never seen that again.

One year, when my birthday came around, Bob had no money to buy me a present. He went to the attic where I kept my childhood dolls and their furniture. He brought them down and set up a little room arrangement on one shelf of a bookcase in our room. He washed and ironed a dress and hat for my favorite old doll and set that on another shelf. I cried when I saw how hard he had worked for his mother's birthday. I'll never forget that special birthday present.

Bob has always been thoughtful. He's loved to bring me flowers. When he was small, he would pick them with practically no stems. For years, I kept an empty salt shaker on the kitchen window for those precious no-stem flowers.

Even the near disasters bring a smile now. One day, I was to take the older children to school. I dressed Bob and put him in the car with the heater on. Then I returned to get the others. The motor was turned on, but the car was in reverse and the emergency brake on. I looked out the window. Not only was Bob missing, but so was the car. Somehow, he had released the brake and the car had rolled across the street and into our neighbor's tree. (There's still a scar on that tree.) If the tree hadn't been there, Bob probably would have rammed into the house.

It was the time of day when many cars were traveling on our street. But God was looking after Bob. We remind Bob that he has been "driving" since he was 2.

Another prank we didn't see as very funny came after Turner had replaced some asphalt tile on our back porch with black adhesive. Even though Turner put the lid back on the can, Bob and a friend managed to get it off. When we found them, they were "painting" the bricks with that black sticky stuff. We worked for several hours to get the adhesive off. Even today some black spots remain.

One experience that Turner and I remember most about Bob was really Turner's error. It involved the loss of a baby tooth. The night that Bob had lost a tooth, the "tooth fairy" nearly forgot to put the money under his pillow. By the time Bob, our youngest child, came along, Turner (the "tooth fairy") was much more generous, and would put a dollar bill under the pillow instead of change as he had done with our two older children. On this particular night, Turner took a bill from his wallet and placed it without turning on the light. The next morning Bob came screaming into our room announcing, "Daddy, the tooth fairy left me $5!" We were as surprised as Bob. And, of course, we couldn't tell him about Daddy's mistake. We still laugh about it often.

Our children were pretty good about not running away from home. I do recall the time a good friend appeared, with John in hand, at our front door. She had spotted him walking down the street many blocks from our home. We asked him why he had run away, and he replied, "I told you I was going to take a walk."

Another time, Bob couldn't be found. All the neighbors searched our area thoroughly. I was making one last round in the car before calling the police when I saw Bob come out of our next door neighbor's house. He was rubbing his eyes. He loved to go over to

Childhood Days

visit our neighbor: this time, however, she wasn't at home and her door wasn't locked. Bob just wandered in and fell asleep on her sofa. It certainly wasn't funny then.

For years, John fixed breakfast for our family each morning. To help him get up and to school on time, his father said he would pay him to cook breakfast each morning. John was paid 10 cents a day plus a bonus on Friday if he hadn't missed a day. He preferred having his daddy keep account of the money and pay him at the end of the school year. Then, Turner asked John how he wanted it, and heard, "I'll take it in big bills." John not only earned money this way, but he learned responsibility, too. And he's a pretty good cook, too.

One of the joys of John's childhood came the Christmas he got a new bedroom set. We kept it hidden 'til Christmas Eve. Turner decided to put up the double-deck bed and all the furniture in the room while John was sleeping. It was risky, but John was a pretty sound sleeper. It worked. When John woke up the next morning, he saw that Santa Claus not only had brought him a new bedroom set — but even put him in the bed.

Maybe it's becauce Betty Cole is the oldest, or maybe she just didn't pull as many pranks, but a few incidents linger in our memories.

When Betty Cole was just 2 or 3, we took a short trip to the mountains, leaving John at home with his grandmother. Turner took us to a lovely old mountain hotel for lunch. All of us were impressed with the array of silver on the table. In the tone that only a 2-year-old can use, Betty Cole said rather loudly, "Look, Mother, two forkses."

Another time, another restaurant: Recently, I had done a TV feature on wigs, noting that people who must wear wigs prefer to call them "hairpieces." At the restaurant, John looked over and saw a lady who appeared to be wearing a wig. In a rather loud voice, he noted just that. Betty Cole corrected him, "Don't say wig. You call them hairpieces." I'm sure that woman heard both John and Betty Cole.

At our first house, Turner always had a garden. It meant good fresh vegetables, and Turner wanted the children to know something about how things grow. One year he planted beans. They were coming along beautifully. Betty Cole thought they were weeds and pulled up each one. Her daddy reprimanded her. So she tried her best to put them back. Of course, they didn't make it.

The children were not the only ones with disastrous experiences. Once, I nearly burned up the kitchen. I was preparing hot dogs by cutting them through in thin slices leaving a small portion of the skin intact. They were then dropped in hot fat and allowed to cook for a few minutes so they would curl. After I put the oil on to heat, some neighbors came to the backyard to take their children home for dinner. In chatting with them, I forgot all about the hot fat. Soon I heard a crackling noise. I went into the kitchen to investigate and found flames shooting up from the pan. The cabinets were on fire. I panicked, and called Turner.

He picked up the flaming pan, took it to the back door and threw it out. If we had just thought to cover the pan with its lid (that lid was lying there just beside it!). Luckily, Turner wasn't burned, but the kitchen was. We had to rebuild the entire thing and clean much of the rest of the house.

Now we can laugh, but at the time these things seemed so traumatic. If I had been away from home more I would have missed most of them. Thank goodness, I could pursue my career and still be at home most of the time.

In recent years, there has been a lot of emphasis on "doing your own thing" and getting out of the home to "express yourself." I certainly agree with some of this. But we should keep in mind a few things about satisfactions and talents.

First, we should look at our capabilities and talents. If you can sing in the choir, it would be a waste of your talents just to work in the kitchen. If you can't speak in public, perhaps you can speak in private by serving on a telephone committee. We don't do anyone a favor by volunteering for a job that we just can't handle.

Usually the things we have a talent for will be things we enjoy. When we moved to Charlotte, I wanted to meet some people, so I joined a club. They asked me to be legislative chairman. "Yes," I quickly said. Soon, I realized that not only did I have no interest in the committee, but I didn't have the capability either.

Another example came in my investment club. The first year, I enjoyed attending the dinner meetings, trying to learn something about stock investing. After missing a few meetings, one member called me and said she would like to bring by the treasurer's books. I asked why, and she told me I had been elected treasurer. I asked what qualifications the members thought I had, and she answered, "You were absent." That turned out to be one of the worst years of my life. Each month, I dreaded for the bank statement to come. I couldn't even get our own bank statements balanced, much less others'.

Time is an important consideration. If you have a family, a delicate balance must be kept between what you do at home and what you do outside the home — and that's for men as well as women.

This I Believe

There is a God. I have talked with Him, hearing Him tell me "Yes" and "No" too many times not to believe. I am a child of God. He cares for me.

God has given me a very special blend of talents, perhaps not as great as those of other people, but my own special blend. He expects me to make the most of these talents in developing them to their greatest potential.

God expects me to make the most of my circumstances. I must learn to accept my handicaps and learn to live with my past mistakes, not complaining but increasing my character by the way I handle these hardships.

God expects me to have proper perspective in my life — putting God and His Kingdom first, my family second, and my career or job or hobbies third.

God expects me to live one day at a time, so that at the end of that day I won't feel I've wasted the precious few minutes that I have on this earth, but have made some small contribution. I must not waste time and energy by grieving about the past nor worrying about the future.

If I can live up to these goals each day, when my time comes to pass on I'll feel that God will be pleased with my efforts here on earth, and that I will have made some contribution.

* * *

When you start writing out what you believe about God, it's sort of hard to say in mere words how you really feel. But I want to outline a few truths in my mind and life.

In church, we recite those beliefs in the Apostle's Creed. Just like we do the Lord's Prayer, we often say the creed without thinking what it means. We are stating that we believe in God, that Jesus Christ is His Son and that the Holy Spirit lives within us to give us direction. This is the Triumvirate. To help us understand, think of a man who is a father, at the same time a son and at the same time a husband.

Many nominal Christians do no more than attend Sunday School and church. Most of us say grace before meals or even read a devotional book daily, but we forget to pray unless we are in trouble or need something. In other words, we try to live as a Christian if it is convenient.

If someone asked you why you belong to a church, would you be hard-pressed to find a reason? Some would confess that is the only way they know, that it's the way their parents lived. We forget that God has no grandchildren — only children. No matter how devout our parents may have been, we need a personal association with God. We must be children of God.

Many join the church, thinking it helps them in business or enhances their social standing, that it makes a good impression to belong to the "right" church.

Even though we study our Bibles, pray and take an active role in our churches, we may be wasting our time. We could compare our efforts to attending a Monday morning sales meeting and finding out all the techniques that will help to make a sale, then not putting those things into practice. We could compare such wasted efforts to a doctor's visit at which he prescribes medicine that we then don't take.

Both Old and New Testaments are full of God's advice through Jesus Christ and the many prophets and leaders in Biblical times.

This I Believe

Lots of wisdom and power are waiting for us if we'll only accept the promises found right in our Bibles.

In those promises written in the New Testament under the Sermon on the Mount, Jesus said we should ask and we will receive. Surely this refers to prayer not only for the things we want and need, but also for daily guidance.

What we pray for may be answered in a way we are not expecting. This anonymous poem from the Civil War expresses our relationship with God through prayer.

The Ways of the Lord

I asked God for strength that I might achieve;
I was made weak, that I might learn humbly to obey;
I asked for help, that I might do greater things;
I was given infirmity, that I might be wise.
I asked for all things, that I might enjoy life;
I was given life, that I might enjoy all things.
I got nothing I asked for, but everything I had hoped for;
Despite myself, my prayers were answered.
I am among all men richly blessed.

I believe God has a better way for each of us. Since He has given us freedom of choice, it's not the only plan, but the best one for us to follow. We must continue to ask His direction and follow His answer, then go on without further questioning what He has told us. This starts early in life and continues with the important decisions of school and job and marriage and staying on the right track throughout our lives.

Many feel life is mostly based on luck. "Being at the right place at the right time" is what some people say when asked how they got where they are today.

In whatever event, we need to set worthy goals. What is your ultimate goal? Happiness is probably sought most. Often, happiness is the by-product of dedication to a more worthy goal.

Fame is what some people look for. But fame is so transient. You can be famous today and forgotten tomorrow. Fame did not make Marilyn Monroe happy.

Fortune is what many people seek. Howard Hughes is a good example of a man of great wealth who dies as a pauper in so many other ways. Surely, this isn't the answer. The 1929 stock market crash is but one example of how quickly a fortune can be lost.

To me, the greatest rewards come through contributing to this world as we pass through. As you inspect your talents and opportunities, you may think you're much more limited than you really are. As you compare your capabilities with those you admire most, do you feel sort of left out?

Even if you can't write a great poem, you can speak kind words to those who need them. Just speaking to someone in a kind of way can lift their spirits for the rest of the day.

You may not be able to paint a picture, but a happy smile on your face may be the very picture that someone less fortunate is looking for that day. As children, we learn it takes a lot more muscles to frown than to smile.

Teach someone something. This is one of the greatest pleasures. In turn, the new lesson may be passed along. These don't have to be monumental lessons; the simplest methods may greatly benefit the right person.

The simplest things — refraining from littering, careful use of energy, not driving too fast, not passing on a critical statement about someone — can contribute to the world, too.

I remember a taxi driver in Honolulu who one Sunday drove a few of us around to find an open restaurant. Finally, he found a quaint restaurant with a very large fish pond (and the largest goldfish I've ever seen). He seemed so interested in each of us and in helping us find just what we needed that day. That was certainly a contribution.

Then there was the baggage man in Holland who searched diligently in the rain for the other half of our tour group of 44 people who had been separated from the rest of us. He made repeated trips to the front of the terminal searching for the bus with the other passengers and their luggage.

Recently I heard of a factory worker who was loved by so many, because he would listen to the problems of his fellow workers with attentive ears and heart as they ate their lunches. Many people are

This I Believe

hungry for someone just to listen. What a simple and beautiful way to make a contribution.

When my life ends, I would like to have it said of me that "She lived in such a way that now that she is not here, it matters that she was here."

Christianity shouldn't be reserved just for Sunday. Every minute of every day can be used.

We can talk to God constantly in prayer. It's easy to beg for help when we feel we really need it and forget God the rest of the time. Thank Him constantly — for the parking place that just opened, the beauty of a seldom seen butterfly, for your child arriving home safely from school, for a safe landing when you are flying and all the other things that add up to a good day.

Driving alone in your car can be a great time to pray. As you're waiting for a stoplight, don't get anxious fo it to change; take that moment to pray for someone. A friend of mine keeps a prayer list in the front seat and uses it at stoplights. Praying aloud and alone while you're in a car is a splendid opportunity to be alone with God. When I do pray in the car, I try to remember to be quiet at stoplights; someone in the next car might not understand what's going on.

So many actvities occupy our days that you can arrive at the end of a day and realize you've spent most of it with "fluff." Check yourself at day's end to see what you've accomplished. God expects us to spend well the precious years He has given us.

Perhaps the most important way to exercise Christianity is really loving those with whom we come in contact each day. That's what Christianity is all about. As we associate with others, we can express our love to each with a smile, or tone of voice, a listening ear, or a mention of our blessed Savior. As we express love for another, more of it comes back to us. It never hurts to tell others you love them.

Cancer!

On my 52nd birthday, I found out that my problems were coming from two malignant tumors — one in my brain, the other in my lung. My doctor asked my family to come to my hospital room at 7 one night so he could talk with us. When he told us about the illness, I really wasn't surprised. After all the tests that had been made, I knew something must be seriously wrong.

The doctor told us that my life might not be as long as normal, but radiation and chemotherapy treatments might arrest the tumors.

I never asked, "Why me?" Instead I thought, "Why not me?" I had often felt guilty that my fortune had always been so good, while so many others seemed to have so many troubles; perhaps it was time for my share.

I knew I had raised a family of three well-adjusted children as well as sharing the love of a very special husband. I've helped educate people in homemaking skills as well as had a chance to let my Christian faith show through TV and public appearances. I have made my contribution.

After the doctor left, my thoughts went first to Turner. How would he get along without me? He's nine years older than I so we had always thought in terms of his going first. Then I thought about our children. Betty Cole was 23 and on her own for a year since graduating from Duke. She really didn't need me as much as she had. John at 21 and Bob nearly 18 were just about grown and could do without me better than several years ago. I thought about my pretty house with all that I have collected and made over the years. I had to admit that nobody else loved those things as much as I do.

Then I thought: "This is ridiculous — I'm not going to die any time soon. I'm going to do my part in helping to lick this thing. God still has important things for me to do." From that moment, about 30 minutes after we were told about the cancer, I've been fighting back.

The story of cancer striking Betty Feezor immediately hit the papers, the radio and television. Did this bother me, someone asked. I said I was glad to be able to let people know what had been wrong with me.

Hundreds of letters and cards poured in. Very few used the word "cancer." Most spoke of my "illness" or "misfortune." Here are excerpts from a few of them:

The Letters

"God's ears must be running over with prayers for you from lots of people. He does answer."

* * *

"I felt bitter toward God that He would let you get sick. Then after hearing you express your views of your illness on television yesterday, I realized how selfish I've been. Thank you for your Christian witness. It means so much to me."

* * *

A minister's wife wrote about a bout with rheumatoid arthritis which left her not only physically sick but in a deep depression for weeks: "For a long time, all I could do was lie on the couch in the den and watch TV. I saw myself as a helpless cripple. I could have faced death more easily, I think. The Betty Feezor Show was one that I watched daily. It was you who inspired me to pick up the crochet hook and needlepoint again, to keep trying even when it hurt."

* * *

Using an example from the New Testament, one viewer wrote, "We've seen your Martha side for years. Now the Mary side is truly appreciated, too."

* * *

Referring to the series of articles I've been writing for The Observer, one reader expressed her feelings this way: "After reading your diary, it makes me feel so selfish to realize that I sometimes find myself down in the dumps for absolutely no reason. You've made me realize that I should be grateful for every moment of my life and not waste time feeling sorry for myself for some ridiculous reason."

* * *

"Congratulations — you're special. God picked you for this sickness because He trusts you. You can view this as a pat on the back from the Lord. God trusts you with adversity."

* * *

"God gives the greatest troubles to those He loves the most and He always gives a way to solve them."

* * *

"God has a special way of using some people and you are one of His brightest messengers."

* * *

"When I learned about your illness, I was so distressed. I've asked the question that so many others have — why Betty Feezor? I've looked at my own life and how little I do for others and wondered why not me instead of her. Then came this week's Charlotte Observer with your first article, and I felt like I knew the answer. I really can't express how it touched me. If I had cancer and wrote my diary, the world would probably never know about it. But through your illness, you are sharing your faith and lives will be affected by it."

* * *

A seventh grader wrote: "I am so sorry about your cancer. But I admire your bravery about the whole thing." A member of my Sunday School class wrote that I write as well as I talk. Another said, "You perk me up like springtime — only better." And another reader wrote, "A good friend of mine recently died of leukemia. If I could have read your articles before, I could have been a better

The Letters

friend to her. If it is my misfortune in the future to develop cancer, I pray that I can face it with the faith and courage that you have."

* * *

Finally from a Sunday School class of retarded: "We are studying about choices, and we thought you made the best choice in accepting God's will. We think your choice will help us and other people make right choices. We hope you'll come back and visit our class again.

Since those first days, I've read and listened and learned so much about cancer. I know, for instance, that your mental attitude has a lot to do with your recovery. One in four of us in this country will get the disease and one in three probably will be cured completely or the disease arrested. Keeping a positive mental attitude goes a long way to help doctors and their treatments work best.

This attitude requires lots of self-discipline. I was tempted to just stay in bed and turn my face to the wall and cry. But that's the worst thing you can do. It's much better to get up, get dressed and back in your routine as soon as possible. Don't forget to rest when you're tired and exercise every day to regain your strength. Though your appetite may not be what it was, you need to eat to keep your weight up, since so many patients tend to lose weight along with cancer.

It's better once you can admit to yourself, then to others, that you have cancer. So many people who have written to me have avoided the word. Many have told me that members of their families wouldn't admit to themselves or their families that they have cancer. Knowing as much as possible about the extent of your disease and the treatment will benefit the patient greatly.

Surgery, radiation and chemotherapy are the generally accepted methods of treating cancer. Even though God is the Divine Healer, He uses these treatments through the skilled hands and brains of the medical profession to cure us.

The treatments often make the patients terribly sick. This isn't always the case. I didn't have surgery, but the radiation and chemotherapy haven't made me sick in these months that I've been treated. If they had, I would have just thought that this, too, is part of the treatment.

In this or any so-called "terminal" disease, you tend to think only of yourself. The sooner you get your mind off your self and onto others, the better for you. People want to know how you are getting along, but most don't want a clinical report. Try to change the subject to how they are getting along and what their families are doing.

Meanwhile, your family needs to make you feel that you can be trusted to do some things you did before. Yes, it's nice to let someone else wait on you in the hospital and at home, but the sooner you return to your former routine, the better off you'll be. Even clearing the table and cleaning up the kitchen can be a welcome "chore" for the patient. When my family and friends stopped asking me every day how I felt, I started thinking I was returning to normal.

In all life's avenues, we need to learn to live one day at a time. We never know when we leave home in the morning if we'll still be here at day's end. Instead of worrying about how much time you have left, make the most of each precious day.

With cancer or any serious illness, face the fact there will be setbacks. On Easter Day 1977 I got the flu. It lasted for 10 days and pulled me back in the progress I was making. In August, my right lung started filling up with fluid rather quickly. So it was back to the hospital for two weeks. Both these illnesses meant I had to start at zero again. But such instances can be great teachers in patience and acceptance of things we cannot change.

One of my most useful lessons is how to cope with pain. Some cancer patients don't have much pain while others suffer excruciating pain with no relief. I have always avoided many drugs, fearing that when I *really need* them they won't work as well as they should. My doctors have reminded me that it is much better to be comfortable and let the body relax without pain. They suggest taking the pain medicine as the pain first appears, and say if you wait until the pain is *advanced* the pain reliever either doesn't act at all or much slower. A great feeling comes when the pain is gone.

Until you've had a lingering illness like cancer, you don't realize how supportive a family can be. Turner and I love each other much more now. He's been more helpful and understanding than I ever dreamed he could be. I've always prayed for his safety every day as he travels, but I'm so much more earnest now in my petitions to

The Letters

Almighty God. I don't know what I would do without him. Many face a long illness alone; my sympathy certainly goes out to them.

Our children are even more attentive than before. Each person in our family is very independent and loving but not to the point of an outward show of affection. Now, for instance, we have longer conversations than ever before.

One person who has been particularly concerned is Donella Mitchell, our maid of more than 20 years. God has touched my life plan here, too. When she first came to work for us, her days were filled with looking after three active children. As they grew up and needed less attention, my mother needed more. Donella was here again to help her in ever so many ways. After Mother was gone and the children were grown and away most of the time, I got sick. Now, she lovingly looks after me.

The support of friends has helped me so much. The love and concern from our friends has carried us right along. Even after many months, people from our church still bring food and flowers. It certainly makes me realize how important it is to remember others who are ill.

I had a hard time learning to be content with a slower pace. At first, I would awaken each morning like a race horse and think, "Now, what do I have to do today." The answer, "Not much," made me wonder how I would fill my day. Having less strength than before limited my activities for a long time, but not my desire for a more active life. Once again, God is teaching me patience and acceptance.

Almighty God is the divine healer. Only He can bring us back to good health. Doctors, with their cobalt and chemotherapy and surgery, can do wonderful things, but these are only God's instruments for healing. When the chemotherapy flows into my veins, I envision the fingers of God working in the cancerous areas of my body.

Other ways heal, too. Instant healing by God has cured many. Who can explain why some get well evidently at the hand of God while others do not — only God has the answer. Death, I believe, is merely a passageway through which we go to meet God. This is the greatest healing, to know there won't be any more suffering or sickness. This, to me, is divine healing.

I have had to sit more than before. Once, I thought how nice it would be to be able to sit as long as I wanted and finish some handwork projects. Or, how nice it would be to sleep as long as I wanted to. But when you can sleep, you can't sleep. At first after my hospitalization, I slept until about 8 A.M. Now I'm usually up by 7 or so.

It doesn't take very long to catch up on the handwork you started before. I feel sorry for people who never developed hobbies that can be done sitting. Reading, stamp collecting, painting, indoor gardening and a lot more can be enjoyed even from a wheelchair. Those still completely active should develop hobbies early in life to prepare for retirement — either voluntary or sudden.

One side-effect of radiation therapy and chemotherapy is the loss of hair. I had been warned of this so I asked my regular hairdresser to prepare an old wig for me. The wig was about 10 years old but it looks very much like my real hair.

Sure enough, my hair started coming out. When my hairdresser shampooed and set it, he told me not to touch it any more than I absolutely must. Several days later, my hair was coming out so badly that Turner suggested I just go ahead and take out the rest. It was very easy. I was left looking like Kojak. Turner thought all this would be very traumatic, but it really wasn't. It was the least of my problems, because this problem could be covered up.

Now I have four wigs to alternate according to how I feel that day. It's a lot easier wearing a wig every day than going to the beauty salon weekly and worrying about sleeping on your hair wrong or getting it wet. Wigs aren't exactly inexpensive, but they are less expensive than a weekly shampoo and set.

After five months, my hair started coming back. Sometimes the hair comes back curly when it was straight before. Often, it is nearer the color of childhood hair. A change in chemotherapy may cause it to come out again.

* * *

What would be your reaction if told you have cancer? Would you just turn your face to the wall and cry? Would you take to your bed and wait for the end to come? If so, it might mean death would come more quickly than necessary.

The Letters

I've come to accept that it really doesn't matter just how much time is left for me, but it does matter a lot, what I accomplish in that time. I've learned not to look ahead to tomorrow, but to live only today. Be grateful for every extra day that God sends to us.

Right after I found I had cancer, I worried about my material possessions. What would happen to all the things I had made and collected for our home? Then I remembered that I should just enjoy each one of them to the fullest each day. I'll follow God's will the rest of my life, no matter how long that is.

I've never believed that God sends any sort of illness to us. I do believe He can use such illnesses to change our lives and give us a new direction. This is what He has done in my life.

My goal has always been making a contribution to this world. God has let me contribute through one of the largest home economics classrooms in our part of the country — the TV audience who watched The Betty Feezor Show daily.

This bout with cancer and having to slow down has given me the opportunity to do less talking and more writing. Soon after I learned of my cancer, the editor of The Observer asked me if I would share my feelings through a "dairy." I saw God's hand again playing a part in my life. Even though well over 140,000 people watched The Betty Feezor Show daily from this four-state area, that's as far as the spoken word would reach. And I was limited to home economics.

Through the written word, my thoughts have gone literally all over the world. Readers have sent the columns to friends all over the United States and to other continents.

Here is a typical letter from an Observer reader in Asheville, N. C.: "I have never heard or seen such positive witnessing under such circumstances. I, in similar circumstances, would have self pity. You are indeed a living saint. You glorify God in your suffering. You are truly one of His children. Faith, hope and love — you have all three."

God has truly given me a different direction. I have been given the opportunity to let people see how I am living with cancer — not dying with it.

The Last Chapter

I wish that I could conclude this book with the fairy-tale statement that they lived happily ever after. Only God knows how long "ever after" will be for any of us.

Here are the guidelines I shall try to follow as I live out the rest of my life, no matter how long or how short:

1. Live one day at a time.
2. Thank God for each previous day.
3. Ask His direction for today.
4. Continue to make my contribution when possible by way of television and personal contacts when I feel up to it.
5. Concentrate more on writing. It is less tiring to me physically. And many more people are reached.
6. Quit thinking of myself and concentrate more on others.
7. Try doing to others as they have done for me during this illness.
8. Slow down and smell the roses; look at God's handiwork in each season. Watch the birds and squirrels from my window.
9. Just sit and feel the warmth of sun and the presence of God.
10. Accept my physical limitations. List in my mind those things I can still do.
11. Learn to take myself out of the middle of my family's activities and thoughts, and take my place as only one of five members of the family.
12. Learn to let other people do for you what you used to do yourself.

I don't know how or when life will end. Whether I get well again or whether God's timetable cuts my life here on earth shorter than expected — either way I win. If my ills are not cured here, they will be in Heaven. After all Jesus has promised many mansions in the eternal life.

God already has healed me long enough to serve others through writing. This book is about my life, career, beliefs, and fight with cancer. I hope it will be inspirational to others.

PART II

BETTY'S DIARY

March 27, 1977

Introduction to Betty's Diary

The most special person I've met recently is Betty Feezor. She has an incredible faith.

These days, Betty Feezor needs all the faith she can muster. She's got a tough fight against cancer of the brain and lung. I pray she wins that fight — she's got so much to offer so many people.

Betty (I don't know anyone who calls her Mrs. Feezor) has been a big TV personality for two decades because of her weekday homemaking show, which ran on WBTV until early February. It was about that time she learned she had inoperable cancer, cancers that could only be treated by cobalt and chemotherapy — and faith.

The odds are, according to medical statistics, that one of every four of us will get cancer someday. It's the second biggest killer, right behind heart disease. Yet it's an ailment most of us are uncomfortable talking about. Did you read that Observer story last month about the cocktail party guests who wouldn't shake hands with a cancer victim, feeling that the disease might be "catching?" Of course, it's not "catching," but that belief, like a lot of other cancer myths, isn't that rare.

Betty Feezor isn't scared to talk about cancer. In fact, she thinks we'd all be better off if we talked about it a lot more.

A few days ago, she and I had lunch at Betty and Turner Feezor's house in Charlotte's Olde Stonehaven section. I had her homemade vegetable soup and the best chocolate pound cake I've ever had. She fixed them both.

We talked about why Betty Feezor is beginning a "diary" in tomorrow's Observer. She hopes that diary, which she'll dictate into a tape recorder, will help you understand what it's like to have cancer and how important faith is in fighting it. After tomorrow's report, Betty Feezor's Diary will next appear the following Monday.

But let her tell you why she's doing this:

"As long as I can remember, I've been a Christian. When I was making decisions like where to go to college or who I should get married to, I'd always pray to God for His help. God has directed every single step of my life. But maybe I never really totally surrendered my life to God until now.

"I was lying in bed the other night, and I was thinking of me, my problems. When I put God in the middle, that just made the whole difference. How can I be thinking of anything else but service to others? From now on, I want to really help others."

Betty Feezor isn't embarrassed by the frontpage stories about her disease. "I thought my public was owed that, to know how I was."

She says she asked her doctor the other day, "Is this gonna get me?" He told her, she says, "There is always hope." And Betty Feezor is a person of considerable hope.

She has been married for almost a quarter-century to Turner Feezor, and they have three children (Betty Cole, 22; John, 21; and Bob, 17). Theirs is a very close marriage, even closer in the past few weeks. "I think Turner loves me even more. I know I love him more. We appreciate each other more."

She finds their children "more attentive. They check on me more. We're real close as a family, but not the kind of family that hugs and kisses. When they heard the news, I didn't see them cry. They just took it."

I've read the first chapter of Betty Feezor's diary. In her own words, you'll find a very special person (she would deny that) sharing a faith from which we can all learn.

Dave Lawrence
Editor, *Charlotte Observer*

March 28, 1977

Cancer Won't Beat Me

It all started before Christmas. I felt pressured with so many activities.

The last four TV shows I did in December I just couldn't seem to think straight. I was nervous. I was losing my self-confidence.

At home, I couldn't seem to write letters very well. I couldn't put my lipstick on straight. I had a hard time writing checks and keeping figures straight.

I talked to my doctor, who thought I just needed to get away for some rest. So in January I took three weeks vacation hoping to get back on my feet and go back to my show. My husband, Turner, took me with him to Atlanta and Myrtle Beach. Both places were very cold and uncomfortable outside, but very comfortable inside with good friends from Turner's farm-equipment sales company. When I got tired, I just went to our room to relax.

I went back to WBTV thinking I could communicate as I had done before — but I just couldn't. I had been thinking for the last two or three years of retiring so I decided to go ahead, and I asked WBTV to end the Betty Feezor Show on Feb. 4.

Turner, who knew I wouldn't be content without something else to do, told me, "You'd better have something else waiting about two weeks down the road. You'll catch up on your knitting sooner than you think."

He was right.

But things didn't get any better. I started dragging my right foot, and sometimes I would fall. In early February, I went back to the doctor, who did a brain scan and found some cloudiness. My doctor immediately put me in the hospital for a week's tests. There, the doctors found a malignancy in my lungs.

The doctor came to my room to see my husband, Turner, and me. Our daughter, Betty Cole, was there, too. He told the three of us that I had cancer. The doctor said my life might be shortened but said we have hope because of cobalt treatment and chemotherapy.

I never asked, "Why me?" Instead I thought, "Why not me?" I've raised a family of three as well as sharing the love of a very special husband. I've helped educate people in homemaking skills and had the chance to let my Christian faith show in everything I do — through TV and public appearances.

I'm not afraid to die. I have to admit that I've always feared cancer more than anything.

When I first heard that I had cancer, I thought, "What will Turner do?" He's nine years older than I, and we always assumed he probably would go first.

Next I thought about our three children. Betty Cole Feezor is 22, John is 21 and Bob is 17. They're pretty grown up now, so they don't really need me as much as they did.

I thought about my pretty house — and the things I have made over the years. But, of course, no one loves those things like I do.

Then I stopped and thought, "This is ridiculous — I'm not going to die any time soon. I'm going to lick this thing. God still has things for me to do. I believe in miracles."

The Effects

I started getting cobalt treatment after I went into Memorial (Hospital) on Feb. 9. The first treatments were in the hospital after two weeks. I know some patients feel a lot of effects from the treatment, but I felt very little in comparison. I started being able to write better. I could put on makeup, and I could think more clearly.

Early this month, my doctor warned me that I would probably continue to feel some effects. He was right. I had a dull feeling in my head and a little more weakness. But I didn't have any nausea at all. My vision is still a little fuzzy at times.

Losing My Hair

I hated to lose all my hair, but the doctor told me it would happen from the treatments. My hair came out as they said it would about a week after I had finished my treatments.

About a week before, when my hairdresser did my hair, he hardly teased it at all because it was coming out so much. He told me not to even touch it. By my appointment next week, it was all gone.

Turner had to go out of town on a business trip. He knew that I was losing all my hair, and he thought I ought to go ahead and take off what hair was left and wear the wig. Turner thought losing my hair would be more traumatic than it really was.

I went into the bedroom and just lifted it off. It didn't hurt.

There was a rash on my forehead as soon as my hair came out, but it went away a week or so later. At first your head gets cold and it is sort of tender, but after a couple of weeks your head toughens.

I knew Turner would still love me even though I look like Kojak.

The night before I started chemotherapy, Turner took me to a wig shop. I wore a scarf. I'm glad no one else was in that shop that night.

We looked at several styles. Turner found a reddish one, which isn't too different from my natural hair color.

He seems as pleased with it as I am. I can work with the wig myself and make it look pretty good.

Because I know I'll be back in TV one of these days, I've ordered a sort of three-color wig that is styled very well.

Not having any hair is the least of my problems. I save the weekly shampoo bill. I could be a blonde or redhead or brownette. When the wig becomes uncomfortable, I can take it off and use a scarf or turban.

Sort of Weak

Even though my treatments didn't make me sick, they did leave me sort of weak. When I came home in late February, I was determined not to give in.

Every morning I get up at 7:30 or so. I dress myself and fix breakfast. I entertain friends who come by. From noon to 2:30, I sometimes sit in my garden room to watch TV — first "Top O' The Day," then "Search For Tomorrow" and "As The World Turns."

At the beginning, I felt very frustrated in not having anything I really had to do before noon and from 2:30 until dinner.

I've learned to read each word of both The Observer and The News. In the old days, usually I just scanned the papers. I read my Bible more. And I've started to read a book about healing given to me by a neighbor who also has cancer. I've learned to read slowly and thoroughly — I have plenty of time.

Some days, I've felt so weak that I learned to just sit and listen to FM or read all those cards that came to the hospital and to our home. There have been more than 4,000 of them. My boss at WBTV, Jim Babb, is helping me by sending a letter to everyone who wrote.

Helping Others

For the first few days I was home, I was letting the whole world center around me. One day, I decided I had to start helping others.

That night I helped Turner get our income-tax figures together. He seemed glad I gave the help.

I took over the check writing and bank balancing again. I started writing notes and making telephone calls.

Telephone calls used to bother me. I had so much to do I kept looking for ways to end the conversation. Now I can talk as long as necessary.

I've called lots of people who are confined to a wheelchair or room. It seems to brighten their days as much as mine.

I've never really been sick before so now it's easier for me to understand others who are sick. I think about how hard it must be to get through the day for people who have to spend most of their working moments in a wheelchair or in bed. People who are blind or deaf — how do they spend their days? So many of them go through such desperate days without a loving family and without enough money. Compared to so many others, I'm so well off.

A Deep Faith

The very night my doctor told me that I had cancer I started fighting back. I've always had a very deep faith in God, which led me to believe He can cure me with the help of the doctors and their treatments. And I've always felt that about 95 per cent of your physical condition depends on your mental attitude.

With my first cobalt treatment, I felt that I was on my way to being cured. As the chemotherapy was injected into my arms, I just knew I was being cured.

And I knew I had a job to do.

Now, when I get up in the morning, I fix myself a big breakfast. For instance, one day I had hot oatmeal, two slices of whole-wheat toast, a big glass of orange juice and some coffee. For once in my life I am thin — in fact at my lowest I weighed only 121 with all of my clothes on. My usual weight is 130. It's so much fun to be able to eat all I want to. I'll have to watch to see I don't gain too much.

Soon after breakfast, I get dressed and put my makeup on. And I stay dressed all day. Many days I go out to lunch so I'm not home.

If I'm home, I eat a good lunch while watching "Top O' The Day." I've learned to eat slowly and enjoy each bite.

For exercise, I walk up and down the driveway. I started a couple of weeks ago with one walk up and back the driveway. Now I'm up to 12 laps each day. It's getting more like spring every day, and I try to spend some time each day working with my roses. If I get tired, I just change activities.

Neither the cobalt or chemotherapy has made me sick. The doctor almost guaranteed that the drug he put into my vein would make me nauseated. But it didn't. I was just terribly weak for two or three days. Even the oral drug, which began a week later (I take six pills every Wednesday and Saturday), didn't affect me.

Beginning March 12, I started regaining my strength and feeling more like my old self.

Each day since then has been a better one.

It's Awfully Important to Feel Needed, Trusted

If you're sick, it feels so good to be waited on and cared for . . . and for decisions to be made for you. But when you start feeling better, it's mentally necessary for you to begin more things by doing more things for yourself. This is good mental medicine.

In the past two weeks, I've felt stronger and I continue to walk up and down the driveway. I am up to 15 trips by now. I can climb the steps from our downstairs den to the upstairs without pulling on the rail quite so hard. I don't feel so tired and weak.

Both our sons have had company recently. Our 17-year-old, Bob, had two choir members spend the night with us. We enjoyed talking to them after they came to our house about 9:30 P.M., and I enjoyed getting up at 6:30 A.M. the next day to get dressed and feed them a good Southern breakfast before they left at 8 A.M. for their next choral appearance.

Unless Bob told them I had cancer, I don't think they even knew. This made me feel I was still able to function as a mother.

Then our 21-year-old came home from N. C. State. John arrived about noon and sat and talked to me for about an hour about school and his fraternity and his summer job. It really seemed like old times.

John asked me how I felt and wanted to hear about my treatment, but we talked mostly about his activities. That's the way it should be.

That night John and Turner cooked steaks on the outdoor grill for the four of us, plus one of John's best friends. One of their favorites is fresh strawberry pies, and I made two of them. I even made a tossed salad with fresh croutons, another of their favorites, and we had baked potatoes.

I cleaned up after we had eaten. And after I finished cleaning up, I felt just about as good as I did before I got sick. I wasn't tired, and I felt I could still function as a hostess and a mother.

Then, the following day, a Saturday, Turner invited two of his business associates for lunch. He seemed pleased with the homemade soup, salad, cheese and crackers and more of that strawberry pie that I served. Even though both men had to know that I had cancer, neither of them mentioned it. It's good medicine to be able to be an interesting wife to my husband's friends.

My Cake Secret

That night we went to a Sunday-school party. I made one of those half-and-half cakes, and everybody wondered how in the world I got half of it vanilla and half of it chocolate. Then I explained about

It's Awfully Important to Feel Needed, Trusted

the little pieces of aluminum foil that helped hold the batter in place until I was ready to put it in the oven.

We didn't try square dancing that night, even though most of the others there did. But we could play some of the other games that were enjoyed at the party.

The next day we went to both Sunday school and church, which was the first time that I had attended both in quite a while. Sunday afternoon, Turner and I went to see the new home of a friend. It added up to a very full weekend, but I didn't feel at all tired when Sunday night came.

Then, on Thursday, March 24, I made my first appearance on the Top O' The Day show since I left The Betty Feezor Show in early February. It felt so good to be in front of the camera again. When Lou Heckler interviewed me on tape before the show and when Clyde McLean talked with me when the show began, I didn't feel any more nervous than when I used to do my regular TV show.

They used a shortened version on my appearance on the early and the late news shows. That way, a lot of TV viewers who were concerned about me could see I was making good progress.

Special Thrill

When you do get sick like I've been, many of my long-standing friends invite you out for lunch. So I've enjoyed getting re-acquainted with a lot of people whom I've known in the past. The other day, I had lunch at the new Radisson. That was a real special thrill.

Last Monday, my articles started appearing in The Observer. Perhaps the best medicine of all for me may be hoping that my reactions to having cancer can help others in the same situation.

I guess what I'm trying to say is that when you deal with someone who has any sort of prolonged illness, it's awfully important for the patient to feel needed. It's just as important that the patient feel their family and friends trust them to do the same kind of things that they did before they got sick.

A friend of mine wrote the other day and said you need three things to treat cancer — faith in God, faith in the medical profession and faith in yourself. No one works without the other. Surely the mental medicine that you give yourself goes hand in hand with the medicine that your doctor gives you and the healing of our heavenly Father.

April 11, 1977

One Day at a Time

I'd like to tell you about taking one day at a time.

Since my last column, I've taped two more television features from my kitchen here at home. I even did a salute to WBT Radio on its 55th anniversary. They asked me to do an ad lib spot — that means no script — for 30 seconds. I did it in 29 seconds, and BT seemed pleased with the spot.

I've had my second chemotherapy treatment. It meant a couple hours of nausea, but I didn't have any weakness like I did before. I think I'd rather have two hours of nausea than two days of weakness. Now I feel just about as good as I did before I got sick.

I've caught up on most of my personal mail. I've put some plants outside — hanging baskets and so forth. Turner and I even pruned the roses.

Cleaning the Closets

Now I'm thinking about cleaning out the closets for spring. But I'm still taking life just one day at a time. When I'm invited someplace, I remind people that I might not feel like it when the time comes, that I may have to call and say I can't go.

I try to remember that I must not overdo. My doctor reminded me that if I do too much, it will break down all the effects of the medication. Of course, I don't want that to happen.

During any long illness, especially when you have treatments, there are good days and bad days. You might as well make up your mind about this right away. Don't worry about the bad days that might be ahead, and try to forget about the bad days in the past. Live just for today.

One Day at a Time

That's what the Bible says.

Remember the 16th chapter of Exodus when the children of Israel were being led to the wilderness by Jehovah? He supplied them a day at a time with manna. Each person could gather a certain portion of manna. If they gathered more than this, it would spoil if they tried to keep it overnight. But, on the sixth day, they could gather and store twice as much manna so they would have it for the Sabbath. This teaches us to take just one day at a time. Jesus warns us not to worry about tomorrow.

A Bit Slower

I've really liked taking things a little bit slower these last few weeks.

For instance, when I take a shower in the morning, I like to stay in there a little longer. I like the feel of that warm spray and I like the feel of the soap, and I like drying off with the towel.

I take more time to dress, and I take the time to look in the mirror like I did when I was a teen-ager so I can decide if *this* really looks good with *that*.

When I clean up after meals, it's fun to give a little extra polish around the sink. My kitchen looks a lot better than it used to.

I like taking care of the mail. Now, I enjoy paying the bills and keeping the checkbook balanced and sending newspaper pictures to friends when they're lucky enough to have had one in the paper. Or just writing notes to people who are not expecting a note from me that day.

More than anything, I like the quiet parts of my day. I try to spend at least an hour studying my Bible, reading some inspirational books, or maybe just sitting still and meditating. This means a lot to me.

Just Delicious

Because I've been a television home economist, over the years I've collected lots of items which have to do with cooking and sewing and handwork. These days I'm trying to use up some of those samples. Our pot roast the other night was made from a chuck roast that came from the beef we have in the freezer. I used a sample of the pot roast mix that came from a package that also included a plastic bag. It was just delicious.

Some of the best salad dressing we've had recently came from another of those packages. I was always too busy to use them in the past.

I've always needed lots of clothes because of being on TV. Now I look at the spring fashions, but I really don't have much desire to buy anything new. As I put the winter clothes away and get out the spring clothes, I feel like I'm greeting old friends again. I'll feel better putting on familiar clothes than going out and buying new ones, or even making new clothes.

* * *

If we learn to live this one day fully, using every precious hour to help those around us, we'll feel accomplishment and joy.

April 11, 1977

Easter Was Very Special This Year

A very important thing happened to me on Easter Sunday when I taught my Sunday school class, the Christian Home class, at Providence United Methodist Church. It did me a lot of good to stand behind the lectern and teach like I've done all my adult life.

The last time I taught, it was a disaster. That was right around the beginning of this year when I had cancer, but I didn't know it then. Anyway, I've always just underlined key words and phrases as reminders. Well, I just couldn't think then, and I ended up reading the whole lesson. I was so glad just to get through it.

This Easter Sunday, I brought my needlepoint sampler, which I started several weeks ago. The sampler says "Christian Home Class." When I got to class on Easter, my husband Turner helped me glue it to the Sunday school class lectern.

Easter Was Very Special This Year

Like Old Times

Our 23-year-old, Betty Cole, came home for Easter weekend. It seemed almost like old times when we went together to the church services.

Some of the members of our church made a rough cross from the trunk and branches of our Christmas Chrismon tree (a tree decorated with Christian symbols). During Lent, it had been bare. Before church, members brought fresh flowers which completely covered the bare branches. It was breathtaking.

That afternoon, Turner and I took a ride and visited with a couple of old friends. It was a very special Easter.

Going to Lunch

My calendar has been so full with luncheons that I don't see much TV around the middle of the day any more. It has been so much fun going out to lunch or having lunch with a special friend in her home.

When I went to my friend, Joni's home, our main dish was a salad that had salmon in it and a lot of other good things. Joni served piping hot rolls, and we had freshly brewed tea and fresh strawberry pie with the most tender crust.

At another friend's house, I had hot poppy seed rolls. Ruth split them, and then she filled them with the best ham salad. And she had fresh asparagus with a good sauce.

We had a delicious congealed tomato salad. I thought you'd like Ruth's recipe. She boils a can of stewed tomatoes. Sometimes, she has to cut up some of the tomatoes into smaller pieces. Then she stirs in a three-ounce package of lemon-flavored gelatin along with two tablespoons of wine vinegar and a few drops of hot pepper sauce.

For a while, I tried to eat as much as my appetite would allow. And now I'm cutting back, especially on desserts. I want to stay at just about the weight I am now . . . 124 pounds. I want to be less than 125.

Getting Better

When I first came home from Memorial, our friends and

neighbors took care of most of our food needs. When I first began cooking again, I depended on tried-and-true recipes.

Now, I'm getting more interested in trying some new recipes. I think this is a positive sign that I'm getting better. These new recipes will give me some ideas for television when I get back to a more regular schedule in a month or two.

April 29, 1977

A Setback, and Time to Reflect

I was planning to talk this time about the food and the flowers, notes and cards which a lot of wonderful people have sent me since I became ill. But some changes have come about.

I developed a persistent fever which stopped my chemotherapy until the doctor can be sure of its cause. I guess those of us on chemotherapy are sort of like hothouse plants: We have to be handled very carefully.

A Step Backward

Of course, I've been disappointed to have to take a step backward after moving forward so beautifully and so quickly.

The first thing I did was cancel all the luncheons and the appointments that I planned on my calendar. This made me realize that I really had been doing way too many things. I thought I was keeping my activities limited to one big thing a day, but now I realize I was working every other minute of that day at something here at home.

The doctor couldn't get the fever down so I finally gave up and stayed in bed for a couple of days, hoping that more bedrest would bring an end to this flu or whatever it has been.

Further Insight

Just lying in bed, with little or no activity, has given me further insight into God's healing. He didn't promise that just because you're a Christian and try to live according to His will, that life will be without its periods of rain or unhappiness. Through the disappointment, God's strength has come through to support me in every situation. And this has given me even more time to read and study and understand.

The thing I had most looked forward to this past week has been the WBTV luncheon to announce the scholarship in my name. Part of the invitation said, "In appreciation and recognition of the outstanding honor and services that Betty has rendered through her profession, the Southwestern Region of the North Carolina Home Economics Association will announce . . . the establishment of The Betty Feezor Scholarship Fund."

Since I didn't feel well enough to attend the luncheon, our youngest son, Bob, stood in for me. He expressed, very well I thought, my appreciation. It pleases me so much to think that some young person will be able to study for a career in home economics under my name.

Practice What I Preach
This setback has made me practice what I've been preaching — there will be good days and bad days. I had prepared myself for that, and I'm hoping that more good days will come along pretty soon.

Taking one day at a time is especially important now during this disappointing setback. We have to make the best of each day as it comes and not look back at some of the bad days or look forward to days which may not be any better.

As a friend of mine, who's a semi-invalid, said to me recently, "This, too, shall pass."

May 2, 1977

So Many Send Letters and Prayers

After about 10 days, my fever finally went down, leaving me terribly weak and shaky. Now my doctor has started my chemotherapy again. Once again, I feel on the road to recovery.

Even now, my friends, and a lot of other people whom I don't know, continue to send cards and letters. And they've brought fresh flowers and delicious food. Caring and friendship means so much to a patient. It's a good reminder for me to remember others from now on.

I've gotten more than 5,000 letters and cards. Many are from overseas — Hawaii, Guam, Africa, even Ireland. These newspaper articles seem to have traveled all over the country. Most of the letters and cards don't even mention cancer. But some tell, in great detail about similar illnesses. The most helpful ones are the short notes expressing concern and love.

Prayers and Cures

Many prayer groups have said they're praying for me. Surely all these prayers together will help me to get well again.

People have sent all sorts of books on healing, and they've sent suggestions for get-well clinics and "sure cures" through natural foods.

Several children have sent pictures; one kindergarten class sent a picture from each child. I particularly treasure the letters I've gotten from many Sunday school groups. The oldest lady so far who's sent a card said she is 91.

People have sent some interesting gifts — for instance tapes with hymns and messages, and things handmade, like an afghan, a pillow, a picture frame. Somebody sent me a room with miniature furniture that was made to look just like the set on The Betty Feezor Show.

When I first got home from the hospital, several church groups brought whole meals. That helped a lot because I really didn't feel much like cooking. The food Turner and I didn't use we put in the freezer for later.

One thing I learned is that when you do take food to someone, it's better to take it in a container that doesn't have to be returned. But if it does have to be returned, it's nice to put your name on the bottom of the container.

Friends Stop By

It means so much when friends drop by. They're very thoughtful about calling before they come to be sure it's a good day to visit. Most of them don't stay too long. I ought to say I've appreciated most of them not telling me any detailed stories of similar illness; that doesn't help very much.

As I look back over the last three months, I think about the love of so many people; I've never met many of these people. People have said, so often, "I love you."

I feel a love and appreciation because I've helped other people through the years. More than anything, I feel a Christian love acknowledging the all-loving heavenly Father we depend on through his Son, Jesus Christ.

<u>May 9, 1977</u>

Luckily I've Found Fashionable Wigs

Every day I look to see if my hair is coming back. But so far, I see no evidence it is.

A neighbor across the street lost her hair and eyebrows because of chemotherapy treatments, but her hair seems to be coming back in. However, as I've said before, the least of my problems is not having hair and having to wear a wig.

Before my hair came out, my hairdresser had fixed an old wig for me.

When I wore it the first time, it looked so full and heavy because that's how wigs used to be made several years ago.

Scissor Work

I decided to cut it down myself, so I just cut away the two pointed pieces over the temples. At first, I didn't think this would hurt the wig at all. But then I looked at the bottom of the back of the wig and saw rows of wig fibers. So I just took my scissors and ripped these out. Now, the wig looks better than it ever did.

But that's not my only wig.

A few weeks ago, I wrote about the reddish wig Turner helped me pick out that has close to the coloring of the hair I used to have. Then I already had another one before I left television and before I found out I had cancer; a wig company had sent me a wig in a television kit matching my hair color. I never had used it but when I needed it, I got it out. It seemed sort of small and close to my head.

I took my comb and found a way to comb it toward my face. The color is rather drab, so I usually just wear it around the house. I can hardly tell when I have it on.

To complete my wig wardrobe and to prepare to do more television, I ordered a wig in a lighter blonde color. When it came, it was so light it looked almost gray. Since it's made from a synthetic, it can't be dyed permanently, but it will take a temporary rinse. Now it's a lovely strawberry blonde. It's styled like I've always wanted my hair to be, but my own hair never has had enough body to fix it that way.

Most wigs have adjustable bands so one wig will fit all head sizes. My head is pretty large, so I cut out the bands to make the wig more comfortable to wear.

Not just wigs make excellent coverings for heads; scarves and turbans work well, too. Large scarves can be folded diagonally; then you can tuck them in at the back if you need to. If you have at least a 22-inch square of fabric left over from a dress that you might be making, you have a good enough size to cover your head completely.

A Mob Cap

One last suggestion is a mob cap like the colonial ladies wore. You might have a bicentennial pattern that would include such a cap. To make one without a pattern, cut a circle 24 inches across, then stitch elastic around the outer edges. Many shower caps are made like this.

One fan of my television show wrote and told me that she has worn wigs for years. To help her wigs stay on, she cuts off the top of pantyhose, then puts this on her head; then when she puts the wig on, it will stick right to the pantyhose and not come off at all.

I feel lucky nowadays to be able to find so many fashionable wigs. I hope some of these suggestions will help you if you have to wear a wig all the time.

May 23, 1977

Slowing down Brings New Pleasure to Life

All my adult life I've tried to take advantage of every waking moment. This bout with cancer has helped me to see that it really isn't necessary to be a machine, always constantly in motion; it's a lot more satisfying to take the time to sit and look and listen to what's going on around me.

One thing I've particularly enjoyed in the past few days is watching the bees that have taken residence in one of our hives. Both of the colonies we had last year died during the winter. But, one day, some new bees came to one of the old hives.

It has been interesting watching them clean out the old hive. Now that's something I wouldn't have taken time to watch before.

I've been busy for so many years, so busy that it hasn't been easy to be less active . . . or at least content to be less active.

Mentally, I will feel better if I have some long-term things to work on. Right now, I have two under way.

First, I'm writing a book. I've written cookbooks before — three of them — and they're pretty easy to do. All you do is collect recipes and arrange them in a logical way. Then, I add some personal comments about where the recipes came from and how my family enjoys them.

Writing an autobiography is a lot different. I'm not really sure just how to go about it. First, I looked at some current autobiographies, and that gave me some good ideas. I've been used to communicating verbally, so I started taping the first chapters. That's much easier than writing in longhand or even on the typewriter.

Then, my second big project is completing a needlepoint front for the handmade lectern in our Sunday school class at Providence United Methodist.

The top part of the needlepoint says, "Christian Home Class," with a small black cross surrounding the blue letters on a cream-colored background. In the lower right-hand corner, I put the date and my intials. The lower part has lettering in the same colors which says, "Living, Loving and Learning With the Lord." We feel that this is what our class is all about. Then, around the lettering, are four birds and four flower designs, all separately spaced.

Each of these two projects will take me a long time to complete. They should keep me occupied while my treatment goes on.

May 30, 1977

Cobalt, Chemotherapy: Instruments for Healing

Good news! I'm responding to treatment. My doctors say I'm making progress. They took some X rays recently of the malignancy in my lung, and those X rays show an improvement from those they took in February. This is the best news I could possibly have.

My doctors have decided that now is the time to interrupt the chemotherapy and administer more cobalt treatments, this time on my right lung. After 10 of these, which will take two weeks, I'll go back to chemotherapy.

The cobalt radiation is like having an X ray taken. The doctor tells the technician where to make some marks in the chest with an indelible pen, marks that don't come off until the treatments are completed. This shows the area where the radiation goes. After the technician gives me the treatment in the chest, she then does the same on my back. They give me the radiation for less than two minutes at a time.

A lot of people feel nauseated after the radiation, but I didn't feel that way after the cobalt treatment for my brain tumor. The only thing I felt was a little dull feeling in my head for a few days. My new treatment hasn't made me sick either. I feel a little weak, but I can still drive to and from the hospital each day.

I've had lots of questions about chemotherapy which they've given me about once every three weeks. That treatment starts with a blood test to get a count of the white corpuscles. If the count is good, a drug is given in the vein, either on the inside of the elbow or, occasionally, in the hand.

As the drug flows in, it feels sort of cold, but it's not uncomfortable. This takes 15 minutes or so, and then they follow that with a bottle of glucose and water to wash out the veins and start getting more fluids into the body. For several days following each treatment, I'm told to drink more fluids. Then, each week I go to the doctor's office for a blood test; nine days later if the count is still as it should be, a second drug — this time, a pill — is taken. I only take these twice a week, Tuesday and Saturday, but I have to take six each time.

This is probably an oversimplified version of what's being done for me, but each person's treatment is tailored for him or her.

The most important thing, all the doctors and nurses tell me, is that you begin your treatments with a positive attitude. That way, they say, the chances are much better that the treatment will work and that the treatments won't make you sick.

As the rays of the cobalt and the chemotherapy drugs flow into my body, I try to think that this is the instrument that God is using to heal me. He is the great physician. He has given the doctors and the scientists the know-how to develop the chemicals as well as how to use them.

June 6, 1977

Feezor Diary Showed the Way

Thanks for the help that I've gotten from your Monday diary. It has really let me see that you can only live day to day.

I have a 16-year-old daughter with leukemia which was

discovered last Aug. 14. She went through the chemo, and a lot of other tests.

Her hair was long, thick and curly. It took only a few days for it all to come out. I prayed, and would cry every time I looked at her without her wig. It was so hard to believe that it could happen.

I didn't live for the Lord, and thought this was my way to be punished. Since I've been following your diary, I've found Him and things are so much easier for me. . . .Since I read your diary and learned to trust in Jesus, she is in remission and getting along fine. She no longer takes the injections, just medication by mouth.

Her hair is coming back good, and the doctors told us Monday that if she stayed like she was now, and her white count stays steady, that she could return to school this fall. Thanks again for helping me see the right way. I hope you have the best of luck in the world.

June 6, 1977

An Understanding Family Helps You Face Difficulty

How do people, I wonder, get through an uncertain time of life, a time unanticipated, without having a family? It would be so much more difficult.

I've written before of my husband Turner, his love and understanding and "Rock of Gibraltar" quality. Because his job is selling farm equipment, and thus he has to travel, Turner often has to be out of town one or two nights a week. But on the days when I have chemotherapy and could be sick, Turner always makes sure he's home to be with me.

Our daughter, Betty Cole, is 23. She graduated from Duke a year ago and now works for a computer consultant firm with offices in Chapel Hill. In her job, she has to do quite a bit of traveling. She thought flying all over the country would be fun and glamorous, but now seems to be getting a little tired of it.

Traveling so much and being so busy, she doesn't get home too often, but she calls frequently to tell us where she is going and to check on me.

Our elder son, John, who is 21, will be in his fourth year at N.C. State next year. He's our outdoorsman. In fact, if State offered a degree in hunting and fishing, he'd surely major in it. This summer, he's really enjoying being a carpenter's assistant for a construction company.

Bob, our younger son, is sort of a "ham," like his mother. He loves to be in front of an audience. He's 17 with one more year before college. Thank goodness!

Both of our boys seem anxious to spend more time at home these days. With permission, Bob comes home to have lunch with me on a regular basis. He often brings friends by in the afternoon to visit.

Donella Mitchell is practically a family member, too. In the past 21 years, she has not only helped raise our children, but looked after my mother for so many years when she couldn't drive any more. She helped me get ready for The Betty Feezor Show most every day. Now, she is as concerned about my illness as my family members are.

I don't know what I'd do without any of them. May God bless us all — and He is.

June 13, 1977

The Greatest Healing of All Comes with Life after Death

When you're confronted with the fact that you have cancer, be prepared for panic and disbelief. You'll probably rethink your thoughts and beliefs.

The most comforting things to do are reading and praying. Those two things, and just communing with God, are the pearls of wisdom that have come to me.

Most importantly, God is the great physician. Only He has the ability to heal. Before healing is possible, we must have faith that

God can and will heal. Unless we have that positive attitude, no healing will come.

Some people experience instantaneous healing. They feel their body miraculously touched and healed by God himself. There are lots of examples of those cured by faith healers, either by physical touching or by prayer.

Don't, say faith healers, lose faith that the cure is real; if you drop back into your old sinful habits, that, too can work against the healing.

Most people use medical healing, such as surgery, chemotherapy and radiation. Any or all of these may be God's instruments for healing. After all, He has given the ability to develop and administer these treatments.

Reading the Bible is very helpful. In the Scriptures, we find out not only what Jesus has promised us on this earth, but also what heaven will be like. Reading inspirational books helps store up truths so we can call on these facts for strength for ourselves and for others. Prayers by others, as well as our own, are important for healing and understanding and peace, as well as strength.

Finally, if such things as medical treatments, prayer, reading from the scriptures and miracle healing don't seem to work, remember that the greatest healing of all comes with life after death.

Then, we will be with our God and Savior. Only then will all our illnesses and infirmities be completely removed for eternity.

June 20, 1977

I Have Memories I Can Call On

If you're limited physically at all, it's easy to be jealous of others who can travel and do all the things you used to do so easily.

When warm weather and vacation time arrive, you start thinking about what you were doing a year ago at this time.

When others talk about where they plan to travel, I think of the trips I've been on in the past. I used to lead tour groups each year so

I Have Memories I Can Call On

I've been lucky enough to go to places like Athens, and Europe and Hawaii. When I see faraway places on television, I like to think that I've been there in that very location.

When others talk about graduation from high school or college, I think of Turner's and my own children. One of the happiest days I can remember is last year on Mother's Day 1976 when our daughter, Betty Cole, graduated from Duke. I still feel real good inside just thinking about it.

When I see a baby in a grocery cart or in a stroller, my mother's heart yearns for those days when our three children were small. Now Betty Cole is 23, and John is 21 and Bob is 17.

I remember the day Betty Cole took some scissors and almost cut off all her little friend's hair. I remember John couldn't pronounce "horse" (he always said "worse"). And there was the time when Bob was 3 or 4, and was home alone with his daddy. Bob had seen me make popcorn lots of times — some corn, some oil, a skillet and the stove set at 375 degrees. So that day, without his daddy knowing it, Bob cooked some popcorn just like he had seen his mother do it. He could have been hurt badly, but now we laugh about it.

But I can't go back to those days, of course. Some day I hope I'll be a grandmother. I just can't wait to be.

I'm not much of a gardener; Turner's more the outdoors, gardening type. But I've always enjoyed my house plants, and I've received lots more since I've been ill. It's fun just to piddle around with the begonias, the geraniums or some other plant. Having plants indoors is a good way to remember how pretty things look when they're growing outside.

We've always taken a lot of pictures, and I've just put them in a cardboard box for years. Now that I have more free time I'm finally going to put those pictures in an album. All the happy faces bring back good memories.

Of course, you can't dwell on the past. There are too many interesting things going on in the present to keep up with.

No matter what your prospects are for getting well, or just improving, there must be many days ahead in which you can find something good. When I find myself getting a little low about not being able to do the things I used to do, I think of the interesting life that I've lived.

I try to remember that even if I never get to do some of those things again, I have built up a lot of beautiful memories that I can call on whenever I need them.

June 27, 1977

Be Positive about Life

Finding out you had cancer used to be the same as a death notice. Today, with treatment so advanced, many of us are being cured or the condition is being controlled for a lot of extra years of life.

In addition to the healing methods I've talked about previously, it's also important to be positive about life and develop self-discipline. Work toward as much of a normal routine as you can. After all, life does go on.

My normal daily routine used to be constant activity from 6:45 A.M. to 11:30 P.M. with few rest periods in between. Now I know that was just too much.

I still get up each day and get dressed just as I used to do when I was on TV every weekday. I feel so much better with my makeup on and my clothes on. And I look better, too. Even if I don't plan to go out, I like to look like I'm ready to go out.

Now, the most important things on my schedule are my weekly treatments and doctors appointments. Then, I need to take care of my family and home. As to TV, right now, I'm doing several TV at-home features every other Wednesday. This gives Top 'O The Day two features every week and means fewer trips to my house by WBTV and less time in presentation for me. It's just as easy to prepare and present several features in one session. We hope to increase the number soon, and I think I'm ready to do some simple commercials, too.

Each day, I set aside some quiet time for reading and studying my Bible. With just so much time these days, I'm a lot more selective about what I'm reading or watching on television.

One good way to make yourself feel better is to cheer up someone who is sick with a phone call, a visit or a note. But don't talk about each of your illnesses. It's a lot more cheering to talk about other things.

Exercise helps, too. When you go shopping, park a long way from the store; that will force you to do that extra walking. Walking around the block or up and down the driveway are good. I try to take 10 to 15 laps up and down my driveway each day.

Resting doesn't always have to be lying down and taking a nap. Sometimes it's restful when I just sit down or do something that is a change of pace.

I've been lucky because I still can do so many things, but there are many cancer patients who are more limited in what they can do. Some require constant care. Some of my suggestions won't apply to everyone.

Many other cancer patients continue to lead very active lives during and following medication. There are pilots who still fly, traveling men and women continuing their travels, volunteers keeping up with their service organizations with unbelievably heavy schedules.

It's so important to feel like iou can participate in things you did before you had cancer. That sort of mental confidence may do almost as much good as anything else.

<u>July 6, 1977</u>

Quiet Reigns, but It's No Time for Loneliness

It was very quiet around our house a few days ago. We got our first taste of the "empty nest syndrome."

Betty Cole no longer lives at home; John is finishing summer school at N.C. State, so he was still away; Bob was a page in the House of Representatives in Raleigh.

Turner and I were alone. With everyone gone and very little to do, Donella even took the week off for her vacation, so the house was really empty.

Turner went out of town each day. In fact, he had to be out overnight, so I had my first experience in many years of staying alone at night. I got along just fine. From now on when I find myself alone overnight, I won't worry about it.

Tuesday, I went out to WBTV and visited my co-workers and went to lunch with two of my special station friends. Wednesday, one of my best friends and I visited a new restaurant; then we came back to my house and did some handwork together.

Thursday, I went to the doctor where I got a good report on my lung. After the cobalt series, the tumor has nearly disappeared. I felt so encouraged I could have flown home; I hardly needed my car!

Friday, one of my former neighbors had a morning coffee for her daughter and invited many of the old neighbors. We had so much fun catching up on what has happened to each of us since we all lived so near one another in the neighborhood.

Then on Saturday, Turner and I went to an 11 o'clock wedding. It was interesting to be at a very formal morning wedding, and also to see another group of friends. It's fascinating to see friends who know other friends, and wonder how they know each other.

Sunday, we went to Sunday school and church. My class, which already contributed generously to the Betty Freezor Scholarship Fund, presented me with a beautifully hand-painted picture with the class member's names signed below. They'd been keeping the picture covered in the back of the Sunday school room where it was signed over several weeks. I hadn't even seen it. Now, it hangs proudly in my garden room where I spend so much time each day.

It has been a busy week. We missed the children, but it was nice for Turner and me to have more time by ourselves. A week without our children home makes us realize there will be lots of good times ahead as husband and wife.

<u>July 11, 1977</u>

I'm Beginning to Feel Like My Old Self Again

Wednesday will be a big day. That's when I'm going to return to public speaking.

I'll be talking to the new Christian Women's Club No. 21 and the

I'm Beginning to Feel Like My Old Self Again

Monroe Christian Women's Club at the Radisson. The Christian Women's Club is an international, interdenominational group designed to introduce Christ to those who may not know Him personally, or who may need a deeper dedication to a Christian life.

The ability to speak in public, it seems to me, is a gift. It comes naturally to most good speakers, but you can build on your ability with study and practice.

Until I got to the ninth grade, I was so timid I was afraid to stand and say anything in front of people. But in the ninth grade in speech class, when I had to do it, I lost my timidity and became confident. Since those days, I've had lots of experience speaking to groups.

In early January, when I had a brain tumor and did not know what was wrong with me, I lost my confidence and felt very ill at ease in front of the television camera, as well as in front of groups. It was a terrible feeling.

Now I have my confidence back. So far, I've taught my Sunday School class one time and done 12 TV features from my kitchen here at home. It has been a good "mental medicine."

Wednesday is going to be special. I'll be standing before 45-women to talk about fabric flowers. This will truly make me feel like I'm back to my old self again.

July 18, 1977

Instead of Worrying, I Count My Blessings

The first 51 years of my life were almost too easy. I was born into a Christian home with loving, concerned parents who gave me everything I needed, including an education that prepared me for an interesting career. Turner and I have never been rich, but we've lived a comfortable life. I've never had to worry about where the next meal was coming from.

Gathering a lot of money has never been one of my goals, but it is nice to have as much as you really need.

I have a loving husband, and we will celebrate our 25th wedding anniversary next month. The rough spots have been few, and we have been able to talk things out and agree on the major things in life.

As our three children grew up, they never really gave us any problems, and they *have* given us a lot of joy. Of course, we had some misunderstandings, but none of the major problems that I read and hear about other people having.

Besides all this, I have had two fulfilling careers that allowed me to express myself, and at the same time feel that I was making a contribution to people. I was a home demonstration agent; then, I was in TV.

All the way along, I felt that God was leading me to do His will. I prayed for Him to lead me as I went along, and as I look back, I can see that He did lead me in so many directions that I never would have dreamed of.

Even my health had been abundantly good. Except for a little back trouble and a bout with hepatitis, I had never really been sick. The only sad times I can remember were the deaths of Turner's and my parents. All of us have these losses, though.

In fact, often I felt guilty that God had been too good to me. Especially when I looked around and saw so many others with really serious problems.

So, on my 52nd birthday when we were told I had cancer, I felt I really couldn't complain.

Who really knows why this happened to me? Perhaps God might be using cancer patients like me as an example to act out our deep religious convictions for others to observe. God may use especially strong and well-known people in this way so others will notice.

Such a serious illness teaches patience, peace and understanding. Instead of worrying about why this happened to me, I count my blessings.

Turn your thoughts toward making the very best use of the days that lie ahead, no matter how few or how many there will be.

Children Cut the Apron Strings

<u>July 25, 1977</u>

Children Cut the Apron Strings

Before I got sick, I had a bad habit of wanting to tell my family what to do about almost everything. If they didn't respond as I wanted them to, it really upset me. When I was in the hospital and learned I had cancer, I started to change. I realized my family could make all those decisions I had thought I had to be in on.

I was thinking about this after we traveled to Chapel Hill about a week ago.

Let me tell you what happened. A year ago John gave up his apartment at N. C. State in Raleigh, just as Betty Cole was moving into her first apartment in Chapel Hill. John's furniture was moved to Betty Cole's apartment; that made a lot of sense since the distance would be much shorter than bringing it all the way home.

Now, Betty Cole and her roommate have moved into a two-bedroom apartment so she wanted her bedroom furniture from home. Meanwhile, John wanted his furniture back at home.

My husband, Turner, and son Bob loaded Betty Cole's furniture on the rental truck. I didn't offer any suggestions about how to do this — I just found old blankets and twine so they could tie down the furniture.

When we got to Chapel Hill, Betty Cole's friends started unloading her furniture. Then they put John's furniture on the truck for the trip home. Turner helped, but the young people seemed to know what to do and where to place the furniture in the bedroom.

I just sat and watched.

Donella Mitchell, our maid, went with us, and I don't know who was more thrilled — Donella or Betty Cole — about seeing her new apartment. Together they fixed lunch, then cleaned up.

I guess I realized then the apron strings had been cut. Betty Cole can take care of herself very well.

On the way home, we stopped to see my sister-in-law. She recently lost her husband and since has had surgery. Her married sons and daughter-in-law were there taking over for her, just as they had done during their father's illness. They had picked beans and tomatoes and had dug potatoes and were freezing and canning.

When we got home, John and a friend started moving his furniture. They set up the bunkbeds and got the right mattress on the right bed. They even rearranged John's room without any suggestions from me.

That day made me realize how special it is to have children who care about you but are independent and can take care of themselves.

I'm thankful that God has let me live long enough to help them prepare for their adult years. God willing, there will be more years ahead to continue to enjoy them.

August 1, 1977

The Doctors Brought Good News and Bad

When I was a teen-ager my doctor discovered a curvature of my spine. But he saw no change in the curvature over time and decided not to do anything to correct it. Over the years, the curvature has increased, and the aches and pains have come more often. In the last few weeks there has been more discomfort, and I've had *very* sharp pains in my left hip joint.

I immediately thought this might be part of a new outbreak of cancer. That's possible, of course, but other things can go wrong with our bodies.

When I visited my doctor for my six-week checkup and told him of the pain, he thought I should have it checked the next week when I visited the doctor who gives me my radiation treatments and checks my X rays to see how I'm doing.

In that intervening week the possibility of more cobalt treatments and the possibility of cancer spreading haunted my thoughts. I prayed I could lay my burden on the Lord and not worry, but I kept slipping back into that same old habit of worrying.

By Sunday, my mind was at rest. Whatever happened, I knew God would be with me. He and I are a majority; together, we can get through anything.

Monday I hardly even thought about my back, though it still hurt sometimes. I didn't know what the X rays would show, but I went to the doctor with hope and faith that whatever the result I could cope with it, with God's help.

My trip to the radiation-therapy doctor brought good and bad news. The bad news is that there is cancer involvement around the left sacroiliac area. My doctor started me immediately on a series of nine radiation treatments. He showed me the "hot spot" on the X ray he'll be working on.

But the good news is that the lung tumor has disappeared. There's still fluid in my right lung, but my doctors hope chemotherapy will clear this up. They also think the brain tumor has disappeared.

I have so much to be thankful for.

This week of worry has taught me it doesn't do any good to worry about what is coming, because there's absolutely nothing we can do to change it. God can handle things by Himself.

<u>August 8, 1977</u>

Misfortunes Can Give Us New Direction in Life

I've never believed that God wills that we be ill or have some other misfortune. None human can explain why a God-fearing person sometimes has so much trouble while a not-so-good person seems to go through life with very few problems. Personally, I believe that God wants the best for us in health as well as in other areas.

Perhaps we have misfortunes to give us a new direction in life. That's happened to me.

Before, my contribution to others came in speaking. More than 130,000 people were in the Charlotte and Richmond TV audiences every day while my TV show was on. It came easy to me. And I felt that I helped many others who were watching me.

Writing isn't anywhere as easy. But God is giving me this

opportunity, and He is putting the ideas and words in my mind so I can put them in print.

Each week I try to think of some idea to help others with cancer or some other serious illness. I try to relate these ideas to my faith in God as well as my own life because readers, just like my TV audience, relate better to everyday examples of family living.

Usually, I write out what I want to say in an old ring notebook left from one of the children's workbooks at school. Then, I read the diary into a tape recorder where it's transcribed at The Observer. If any changes are needed, either Dottie Adams or Dave Lawrence calls me from the paper to make sure I approve.

The printed word reaches further than the spoken word. Mail has come from all over this country and from many people overseas who have read the articles which were sent to them by friends in the Charlotte area.

Even though the spoken word reaches many people, it has a limited area of coverage. The printed word can reach just as many people, but in a much wider area.

Surely God has this in mind as He is healing me for perhaps a greater work ahead. He's using my illness to give me a new direction.

August 15, 1977

It Was a Busy Week . . . It's Nice to Slow Down

Our family has had a very busy week. It began with selecting furniture for Betty Cole's old room which now will be a home-office for Turner. We shopped several stores before making our final decision. Turner and I had fun doing this shopping together. We haven't done something like this in a long time.

A week ago Sunday, my sister-in-law visited from Davidson County, near Lexington. Because Mae had surgery on her foot recently, she enjoyed just sitting most of the time. Her son and daughter-in-law brought her down and they stayed for dinner with us. For dinner, I tried out a new recipe for curried chicken salad that I'll be using on TV soon.

I finished up my cobalt series on my hip joint on Monday, Tuesday and Wednesday. The treatment didn't make me sick or weak, so I could continue to enjoy our company.

Wednesday night was really hectic. That furniture was supposed to arrive at 1:30 in the afternoon, but it didn't come until around 6. Meanwhile, a friend of John's arrived and we invited him to stay and share our pork chops. While I was setting an extra plate, the furniture men discovered that the large desk we had just bought wouldn't go through the door and down the hall to the former bedroom. So, it had to be reloaded.

This was the only time during the week that I got tired — perhaps, tense would be a better word.

Thursday, Turner took Mae home, Betty Cole went back to Chapel Hill, John left for the beach and I kept my doctor's appointment for that morning. That afternoon, I did my usual taping of three TV features.

Friday, I had the whole day off, and Bob was working. It was nice to have a little peace and quiet.

Before I got sick, such a busy week wouldn't have been unusual. When I gave up my TV show, I missed all that acitivity. It took me quite a while to slow my pace and to fill my day, but I have learned.

It was so nice to be involved with my family and feel that I was back in full swing again, but it was also nice to slow down. Whether you're sick or not, find a pace to function well but still have time to stop and smell the roses.

August 22, 1977

Many Dread the Thought of Cancer

Three doctors treat me on a regular basis: one is my doctor who discovered I have cancer, another does my radiation therapy and the third directs my chemotherapy. They keep in close touch with each other. One tends to be optimistic, one rather pessimistic and the third is sort of in the middle — which gives me a well-rounded look at my case.

One of my doctors explained to me the research into how a combination of drugs may help cure cancer in the most people most of the time. Another explained how the balance between radiation treatment and chemotherapy is a very delicate one. So far, the results of the research are not all in; the medical profession has to try one combination of drugs and then switch to another to see which is most effective with each patient.

After the last radiation treatments on my hip, they decided my chemotherapy should be changed. Chemotherapy works throughout the body and can cause side effects such as loss of appetite, nausea and loss of hair. In fact, 80 percent of the patients on this new combination of drugs lose their hair.

Of course, my hair came out after radiation treatments on my brain. It's coming back in, but it may come out again, according to my doctor. The change of drugs did not make me nauseous, though; in fact the next day I went to lunch at a friend's house and ate every bite.

One doctor, new on my case, asked me how much I knew about the extent of my condition. I told him I thought I knew everything, but if I didn't to please tell me. He told me of many people who would rather not know or whose families don't want them to know. One hospital he had worked in put colored tapes on patients' folders to guide doctors in just what to say to each patient. Many people dread the thought of cancer so much they cannot admit even to themselves that they have it. Some never say or write the word.

I believe the sooner you can admit to yourself what your problem is and bring it out in the open, the better off you are.

When people ask about your progress, they don't need a clinical report. But lots of people really are interested in just how cancer treatment is carried out. Usually, answering their questions simply and then changing the subject is good procedure.

August 28, 1977

How Would YOU Respond to Cancer?

Yes, we're all terminal.

In the past couple of weeks, I've read about the deaths of such people as Groucho Marx and Elvis Presley and Sebastian Cabot. Their deaths and so many others remind me that death can come at any age. We are all terminal.

Sen. Hubert Humphrey was told that he has an inoperable tumor and that he can expect to live several months or several years. From what I read, he first reacted with despair but then began looking forward to starting chemotherapy again, and returning to the Senate to finish up some important work.

What would be your reaction if you were told you have a terminal illness? Would you turn your face to the wall and cry? Might you want to just give up and take to your bed and wait for the end? That sort of thinking might mean death would come more quickly than necessary.

Some people stop work and just indulge themselves — traveling, or buying a lot of clothes, or maybe a boat they always wanted and never had. As the saying goes, "Eat drink and be merry, for tomorrow you may die."

Personally, I have come to accept the fact that it really doesn't matter just how much time is left for me — but it does matter, a lot, what I accomplish during that time.

I have learned not to look ahead to tomorrow but to live only today. We should be grateful for every extra day that God sends to us.

Right after I found out I had cancer, I worried about my material possessions. What would happen to all the things I had made and selected in our home? Then I remembered that I should just enjoy each one of them to the fullest each day as if I were going to live for many more years and be able to enjoy them.

I'll continue to follow God's will the rest of my life, however long that may be.

Making some contribution to this world has always been my goal. So far God has allowed me to do that through one of the largest home economics classrooms in this part of the country — my TV show.

Having to slow down has given me the opportunity to write my innermost feelings which I wouldn't have been able to tell you about on TV. My motto has always been to live so that when you're gone, it will have mattered that you were here.

Whether you have a terminal illness or not, today is a good day to check what you're contributing to others, to life. Who knows when life will end? God's timetable may not match ours, but His is perfect.

September 5, 1977

After the Pain, There's Relief

I'm doing this diary from a hospital bed where they're treating me for fluid accumulation between my lung and my rib cage.

For several months now, I've had a tightness in my right side that hurts, especially when I sneeze or cough or just breathe deeply. In the past few days, it got a lot worse. I had trouble breathing. X rays showed a rather sudden buildup of fluid.

My doctors put me back in the hospital to try to remove the fluid. First, they injected Novocain to relive the pain. Then, they inserted — using an x ray to guide them — a needle between my ribs. For the next 10 minutes or so, they drained off the fluid into suction bottles. About a quart and a half of fluid was taken out, so it's no wonder I was so uncomfortable.

The doctors kept me in the hospital for the next four days to see whether the fluid would return or not. Then they took another X ray to see if the fluid had returned. It had, to some degree, so they inserted a tube to try to drain it completely.

Meanwhile, they're giving me chemotherapy for not only the affected area but also throughout my body.

Any time the body malfunctions, there's a certain amount of pain.

I've always tried to stand the pain as long as I can. Then, when the pain is gone, there's such a sense of relief at being back to normal.

I like to think of it as an act of faith, asking God to help relieve the pain instead of depending on pain pills. Then, too, if there's more pain ahead, those pain relievers will do more good if you have not built up a resistance.

As God tells us, He does not send more trouble or pain than we can bear.

<u>September 12, 1977</u>

Men and Women in Medicine Heed a Special Calling

I'm home again now, but my stay in the hospital lasted longer than the two or three days I expected. After the doctors removed the fluid from my rib cage, more fluid returned, so they did a second procedure in which a tube was inserted between my ribs. It didn't hurt much when the tube was put in, but it got very uncomfortable, espcially when I was lying on my right side.

Several hours later, a strong form of chemical was put in the tube as part of my chemotherapy. At first it didn't hurt. But in a couple of hours, I was in real agony, so they gave me some pain shots.

The fluid ran into a jug on the floor. Turning from side to side brought a great deal of discomfort.

In midafternoon, my blood pressure dropped drastically, so they began a glucose and water solution in my right arm. That night, I was awakened every four hours so my blood pressure could be checked.

Very early in the morning, a thoracic surgeon removed the tube. Almost immediately, I started feeling better. I ate a big breakfast of juice, cereal, scrambled eggs, toast and jelly and coffee. All my vital signs were back to normal.

My stay at Memorial has helped me see several things. For one, I see so many people much worse off than I.

And I have seen the concern and hard work of the doctors and nurses. The surgeon who removed the tube from my side arrived at 5:45 A.M. Other doctors often are here before 7:30 A.M., sometimes returning as late as 7 that night. The nurses are all so dedicated and seem to run from one duty to the next.

Surely there is a special calling for all the men and women in the medical profession. Even though God is the divine healer, these dedicated people are His servants and the instruments of His healing.

My illness has made me so thankful for friends who care and for those people who have never met me and yet express their concern.

I'm especially grateful to a lady in Australia who sent the box of cake mix. Now that I'm home, I'm looking forward to making this genuine Australian cake.

September 20, 1977

Family Brings Appreciation

What a difference two weeks can make. After time in the hospital, I find so many things have happened while I was away.

First, I learned that two weeks in bed can really tire you. Now that I'm home I have to sit or lie down once in a while when I feel tired. Just walking around was an effort at first, but now I'm feeling much stronger each day. I'm climbing the steps more easily now.

My doctors and my family have warned me again that I must not push myself. Thank goodness for books to read and handwork to do and this diary to write each week, as well as my autobiography to finish. All these things help fill the hours. I may be physically tired, but the mind is always active.

I learned to appreciate all over again my family and all the things they do for me. Our maid Donella Mitchell fixes all or part of our dinner each night; Turner and the boys put it on the table and do most of the cleaning up afterwards. But I keep insisting they can't load the dishwasher as well as I can.

It Takes Time to Get Used to Slow Pace

John is not attending N. C. State this fall semester, so he and Bob are home most of the time except during work and school hours. They are so much company to me, which they've always been, but it seems so much more important now. Perhaps it is part of God's plan for us to have more time to be together.

Betty Cole flies to Chattanooga and/or Chicago every week on business. When she can, she stops over here for a day or a night; she calls every day or so to check on me, too. She's turned into quite a cook. On her last trip home, she made excellent chili and the most delicious homemade croutons for the salad.

Friends have started all over again bringing meals and calling to see how I'm doing. They seem content to just check with whoever answers the phone, instead of calling me to the phone. What would we do without friends!

When I was in the hospital, I quit taking so many beautiful things for granted. Now I see that our recent rains have turned all the brown grass and trees and plants ever so green. Freshly mowed lawns seem even lovelier.

One afternoon, I took some time just to watch a couple of squirrels scampering around the patio. Perhaps they were playing, or maybe they were gathering nuts for fall. There were also two bluejays that screamed and flew back and forth at each other.

There is so much natural beauty to be enjoyed. Often, all it takes is a little slowing down to let us appreciate the beauty of God's earth and the love of our family.

<u>September 26, 1977</u>

It Takes Time to Get Used to Slow Pace

As the years go by, the life expectancy of men and women seems to be getting longer. Meanwhile, people are talking more now about allowing both sexes to work longer. A lot of people nowadays think 65 is too early to end a career when they still have so much to offer.

You, of course, need to plan for retirement long before you

actually retire. If you develop hobbies and outside interests early in life, it will give you something to occupy your time later on.

But how does this all fit in with having a serious illness or terminal disease? More than you might think. It's not uncommon that some of us must, because of illness, forego our active lives for one much more physically limiting. Some of us are "lost" at such times, because we're not mentally prepared to change so quickly.

Some of that happened to me when I first learned I had cancer and consequently would have to spend so much time inside. It was quite an adjustment!

Could I be content to do less running around and more sitting and occupying my mind in other ways?

It really doesn't take very long to read the paper from cover to cover, to read all the magazines that come and to spend an hour or so in devotional and Bible reading and prayer. It didn't even take me long to catch up on all the knitting and cross-stitch and crochet projects I had started.

Since March, I've finished two needlepoint pillows and made a needlepoint cover for the front of a lectern for my Sunday School class. Now I'm working on a latchet-hook wall hanging for a Christmas present, and I've ordered other kits to keep me occupied well into the Christmas season.

I'm lucky I enjoy doing handwork. I hope others learn to enjoy it, too.

Recently, a friend proudly showed me some handmade afghans her husband had done. Before then, he had never held a crochet hook. An airline pilot I know does a dainty cross-stitch. Recently I read about a young lady, completely paralyzed except for her head and neck, who taught herself how to paint. We read about people who do remarkable things from wheelchairs. I even heard of a beauty contest for people confined to wheelchairs — beauty of spirit, that is.

After two weeks in the hospital and then two more weeks of feeling slightly under par, I have learned I can be more content a little longer each day to just sit and look out the window or talk to my family. I don't *have* to do something every second.

Even waiting in the doctor's office can be interesting if you just watch the other patients who are waiting.

Thankful for a Day Away, a Double Rainbow

We never know when sudden inactivity may confront us. Don't be a workaholic — develop some other activities to call on to fill those hours.

October 3, 1977

Thankful for a Day Away, a Double Rainbow

It's been several months since I've been out of Charlotte even overnight. But a few days ago, Turner had some business in the mountains and invited me along. Those were two days I'll always remember.

We started with a leisurely drive to Lenoir where Turner called on two customers while I sat in the car and enjoyed the gentle breezes and read that morning's Observer and a book, "With Each Passing Moment," by cancer patient Mary Higginbotham. It was so nice to have no responsibility, other than just being Turner's wife.

We enjoyed a light lunch in Lenoir, then drove on up to Blowing Rock. Although the skies were clear when we left Charlotte, by the time we reached Blowing Rock it was raining. We found a room in our favorite mountain-top motel. Then, while Turner made more sales calls, I took a nap.

The rain outside and the security of the beautifully decorated room gave me such a feeling of well-being. Knowing there was nothing I *had* to do and that Turner would be back soon to look after me gave me a special warm and protected feeling.

We had camped often at Julian Price Park a few miles outside Blowing Rock in years past, so we drove over to see what it was like this year. We found very few campers on hand. As I saw the few campers brave enough to pitch their tents and cook in the rain, I was very glad that we could stay in our nice dry car, eat in a lovely dry mountain restaurant in Boone and go back to our nice dry room for the night.

But it was fun for Turner and me just to talk about all the good times we had during our camping-out days.

On our way back to Boone, we saw our first-ever double rainbow which reached from horizon to horizon. It was so beautifully complete that we stopped the car and got out just to take in all that beauty. Both of us are sure this double rainbow will bring us double good luck.

After a family-style dinner and a mountain-size breakfast, we drove on to North Wilkesboro. The trees were beginning to change color. The weather was crisp and cool and there was almost no traffic. During those 30 or so miles, I tried to take in everything to keep with my memories of near-perfect days.

I have so much to be thankful for.

October 9, 1977

Betty Feezor's Prayer

Gracious Lord, how great Thou art!
How great Thou art for providing this beautiful world in which
    we live.
How great Thou art for sending each of the four seasons—
    especially Fall with its beauty of color.
How great Thou art to give us the assurance that You care for
    each of us.
How great Thou art to provide a plan for each of our lives;
    not the only way, but a better way for us to fulfill
    Your will for us.

We pray for those who are old and lonely. Reassure them that
    You love them when others may not.
We pray for those who are poor in material things. Give them
    faith that miracles still happen, that things can improve.
We pray for those who are poor in their spiritual lives. May
    they find a deeper faith in You.
We pray for those who are in prison — not only behind bars,
    but in the prison of a wheelchair, or the prison of feelings
    of guilt or fear.

Think First of the Sick When You Go Visiting

We pray for those who do not really know Christ. May You fill us with Your Holy Spirit as our constant guide and counselor . . . AND

May we not be so concerned about the length of time that we may have on this earth. Let us make the very best use of each precious day. Help us remember that Your timetable is perfect. How great You are not to let us see into the future or to know when our end of time on this earth will come.

And, oh yes, Dear Lord, let us not forget that we are Your disciples as surely as the first twelve. Help us to take advantage of the opportunities we have for telling others about Your precious Son.

All of these petitions we send to You in the name of Your Son, Jesus Christ. Amen.

— Given at Providence United Methodist Church
Charlotte, North Carolina

October 13, 1977

Think First of the Sick When You Go Visiting

Have you ever felt guilty about not visiting someone who is sick?

Maybe you're doing them a greater favor by not going. There are other ways of letting a person know you care other than actually visiting.

If possible, call to find out if the patient feels like having company. Some days you may feel so bad you don't even want your own family to see you. Calling in advance not only will help check the well-being of the patient, but also give the patient a chance to freshen up a bit before you get there.

Don't stay too long. Even though the visitor may do most of the talking, it can be very tiring to the patient. A half-hour is usually long enough.

When you have been sick, you'll be weaker than usual. Beware of visitors who hug too tightly. (Besides, often a handshake is more sanitary.) If you're standing, some visitors continue to keep an arm around you, not realizing that sort of excess weight can tire you even more. It could even make you lose your balance or lose your wig (I've been wearing one since I lost my hair after cobalt treatment). Watch out for those who hug too hard. Losing a wig could be embarrassing, not only to the patient, but also to the visitor.

When you're talking to the patient, stand or sit in front of him or her. Some visitors stand or sit to the side or the back, causing the patient to turn his head in an awkward position. Try to place yourself on the same eye level as the patient.

After an illness, too much noise and too many people may be bothersome. That's one good reason that hospitals allow only a few visitors in a patient's room at one time. If you are visiting and another visitor comes in, perhaps you ought to leave.

A visit to a sick person does not require your taking a gift or flowers or food, but it's nice to do. But a gift sometimes can be a burden — like taking food in a container that must be returned. If you do take something in a container that needs to be returned, be sure you have your name and address on it. Better still, say you'll come back and pick it up at a later date.

The same goes for flowers; the patient will probably appreciate them much more knowing the vase doesn't have to be returned. It's nice to keep some inexpensive containers on hand — maybe those you have received as a patient yourself. Put a note on the bottom: "Please do not return." If you take a gift that would require a thank-you note, do tell the patient a note is not necessary. Writing a note for some people is as painful as the sickness itself.

We all appreciate the thoughtfulness of people which people express in so many ways. The added thoughtfulness of some of the ideas I've mentioned will make the appreciation even deeper.

October 23, 1977

How Good It Is to Feel Good

There will be good days and bad days, good weeks and bad weeks. That's what my doctor said when he told me I had cancer.

Most of mine have been good so far. I have been relatively pain free; neither cobalt nor chemotherapy has made me sick.

When I feel pain in my back, I always think it's due to the curvature of my spine. This wasn't the case back in early summer when pain in my left hip turned out to be a spot of cancer. A series of cobalt treatments cleared up that, so I've not been bothered by that hip since.

Then there was some discomfort in my right shoulder; the scan showed that to be more cancer. We decided not to treat this with cobalt, but to see if the chemotherapy would take care of it. That must have happened, because I haven't had any pain lately.

Suddenly about two weeks ago, I was drying my back after a shower when the pain hit my left shoulder blade. I thought I had pulled a muscle. When I saw my chemotherapy doctor, he said it might be another cancer spot. After a week of taking pain pills and making sure I wouldn't strain my back, we decided on another series of cobalt treatments. When I think back, I remember now that I was tired and feeling pain at that spot several months ago.

When I look at my latest bone scan and X rays, it seems some spots have decreased while others have appeared or just held their own. I'm still optimistic.

Both my doctors think chemotherapy eventually will clear up these spots. I've not had any more fluid problems. And the brain and lung tumors seem to have disappeared. I feel I'm making progress.

Right now, I'm taking more medicine than I wish I had to. Some side effects seem as bad as the effects of the cancer itself.

My kitchen window sill looks like a miniature medicine cabinet. One medicine irritates my stomach. Another leaves the inside of my mouth very tender. My pain pills make me drowsy. This cobalt series has made me slightly nauseated.

I've always hated to take medicine unnecessarily, but my doctors remind me that pain relievers do a lot more if you take them when the pain starts instead of waiting until its severe.

Maybe God is using these discomforts to help me realize how good it is to feel good after a bad day or a bad week. He has many lessons to teach.

November 1, 1977

Savoring the Beauty of Autumn

Last week found me finishing my cobalt treatments on my left shoulder and getting my mouth back to normal again (medication had left it very tender) with B-complex vitamins plus a special mouthwash. My blood count was still low.

As the week passed, I continued to feel better. Betty Cole came home with a former college roommate, Jenny, and we were glad to see her again.

For supper, I made a layered salad (lettuce, onion, bacon, cheese and green peas mixed with mayonaise). Jenny described for me the new "dig-down" salad that her mother had just discovered. It was almost like mine. That shows that whether you live in Pittsburgh or Charlotte, new recipes are pretty much the same.

Our son, John, spent most of his week hunting. He came back very pleased to have shot his first deer with a bow and arrow.

Son Bob spent most of his week rehearsing for his senior class pageant.

It was a busy week for our whole family.

Saturday night, we visited the home of some of our dearest friends for an oyster roast. The next day after Sunday School our cousins from Lexington came down for dinner. We went to brunch in uptown Charlotte.

After brunch, Turner drove us all around Charlotte. That day you didn't need to drive to the mountains to see the color — we had plenty of it right here. We saw that when the sunlight hits the leaves, even those that look pretty flat and drab take on a special glow.

Some people seem to have the same quality. It's as if the sun shining through them escapes in smiles.

The leaves had begun to fall. We all thought the color looks like a carpet beneath the trees. Maybe this is just our excuse not to have to rake the leaves so often.

We are fortunate to have four seasons here. The colors of spring are light and tender, reminding us of babyhood. Summer brings on bold and bright colors; they remind me of the brashness of youth. The fall colors are deep, and they tell me of maturity. Winter is beauty, too; the world sometimes seems to go to sleep until spring revives it again.

These beautiful fall days remind me even more of how gracious God is to provide such a magnificent world. Each day of each season is precious.

November 7, 1977

It's Time for Bringing the Things We Love Close By

The only symptoms remaining since my reaction to all the medicine I've been taking is a very dry throat and cough. My doctors tell me it takes about two or three weeks after radiation therapy for the effects to go away. In the meantime, I've had to talk softly, if at all.

About the same time my cough started, we learned from our across-the-street neighbor that two of our tallest pine trees had died. The trees were so tall we couldn't see the tops very well from our yard, but they were evident from across the street. While I watched the operation from a safe distance, son John used his "climb-the-tree" deer stand to fasten a cable near the top of the shorter of the two. Then Turner used his power saw, while John and Bob pulled on the cable. They managed to land the tree on the driveway instead of on other trees or the house, but they had to get a professional to cut the taller tree, who had it down in minutes and in a few more minutes had it cut into logs.

When I went back to look, all my neat, tidy, organized mind could see was a huge mess that looked beyond ever being cleaned up. Turner said all he could see was a lot of good fires for winter. After two weeks of chopping and hauling and stacking, the front yard is back to normal, and we have plenty of firewood.

We already have brought in most of the plants we want to save. (Some I have shared with friends and neighbors; Betty Cole took some with her for her apartment and office in Chapel Hill) I have to remember not to overwater them, because I understand plants go into a dormant stage this time of year and don't need much water or fertilizer, especially if they're in plastic pots. Baskets that have been hanging on the porch may now hang in a window with the same exposure, but you may need to trim them back, rooting some of the cuttings for next spring.

I have some begonias that have been thriving in the same pot for years, so I can pass on several ways of saving geraniums until next spring. The first is to bring the pots in to a very sunny window, after cutting them back; they usually will continue to bloom. Or you can place them in a not-so-sunny basement window, watering them about once a month but not fertilizing them. Or you can just pull them up by their roots and lay them directly on the dirt in an unfinished basement or under the house, being sure the roots touch dirt. By spring, new shoots will have come up, all ready for planting.

Another thing to bring in at this time of the year is the sun. Look around and see how its position has changed since summer. You may be keeping out the sun's warm rays with shades and draperies. Uncover the windows and fill them with plants. See if you can't arrange a chair and footstool in front of a sunny window for reading or doing handwork.

When we were looking for ways to save energy a couple of years ago, several of my TV viewers sent me ideas. One had put her sewing machine in front of a window instead of in a dark corner with a light where it had been before. She could see even better this way and save electricity at the same time.

Bringing in the outdoors with blooming plants, sunshine and firewood close by add up to a cozy and comfortable fall and winter. It's the same with the limitations we often have with a long illness, bringing the things we love close by since we have to stay a little closer to home. God is always there to help us compensate for the limitations we have and the changes that come about in our lives.

<u>November 14, 1977</u>

My Pinch Hitters Come Through

When I first found I had cancer, I decided that each day is so precious I would use it as carefully as possible to finish carrying out God's will for my life. Not long before, I had given up my TV show, so I still had the feeling of a racehorse inside the body of a turtle. I wanted to say yes to so many social and speaking engagements; that's what I had always done before.

Slowly but surely God has been teaching me patience. I've learned to say no to many invitations. And to those I've accepted, I always add; "So far as I know now, I can do it. If I don't feel like it at the last minute, I may have to call and cancel."

To fill some invitations, I've found a substitute. In April the Home Economics Association established a scholarship fund in my name for home economics students. A lovely presentation luncheon had been planned. Hard as I tried to feel good when the day came, I just didn't feel up to it.

Bob, our younger son, took my place and accepted the honor. He was a good stand-in.

In August, the N. C. Chapter of American Women in Radio and Television gave me a plaque pointing out the years of leadership that I had given to women in television. That day I did feel good, so I appeared on the Top 'O The Day show to accept the award.

Then this month the North Carolina Home Economics Association gave me its first award to a home economist teaching through televsion. Knowing I hadn't been up to par for the past several weeks and couldn't stand the trip to Raleigh, I asked our daughter, Betty Cole, to stand in for me. She asked her brother, our older son, John, to go with her. Betty Cole told the audience how much the association had meant to me and how much I would appreciate the plaque. Then Betty Cole told them she still couldn't cook even though her mother was a home economist.

Husband Turner has not stood in for me the way our three children have, but he has taken the responsibility of talking on the telephone to friends who call and ask how I'm feeling. He helps me decide what I'll do and what I won't do.

But best of all, you should see Turner and the boy stand in for me with dinner preparation and cleanup. They've really surprised me with how efficient they can be.

All this standing in makes me realize perhaps I had been taking too much responsibility and not depending in my family enough in the past. They have surprised and delighted me with their eagerness to stand in.

A lingering illness certainly can bring a family closer together.

November 21, 1977

Mom's Advice Stands the Test of Time

THIS ARTICLE WRITTEN BY
BETTY COLE FEEZOR, BETTY'S DAUGHTER

The expression "like mother, like daughter" has never been particularly true in our family

Mother and I have entirely different educations, careers and lifestyles. She attended the University of Tennessee and majored in home economics; I graduated from Duke (where home economics is not even taught). And, to her bewilderment, I majored in computer science and mathematics. Mother has never understood how she could raise a daughter who is a mathematician when she failed algebra twice.

Mom's Advice Stands the Test of Time

Mother has had a lot of success in TV, public speaking and homemaking, while I work as a consultant for a management consulting firm that designs computer-based planning systems.

Mother lives with the rest of my family (my dad, Turner; brothers John and Bob) in Charlotte; I spend most of the working week in various airports and hotels around the country and live in an apartment in Chapel Hill on weekends.

As Mother fights cancer, she continues her lifelong dedication to helping and teaching people by writing her articles for The Observer. What I'd like to tell you about are Mother's most helpful lessons — guidelines I follow at my job every day:

- **Be Honest:** All those years Mother was on TV, she was never afraid to show her failures. If a cake burned or a souffle fell, she would show it on air and admit her mistakes. I just know this was one reason for her success, and I think honesty applies to the business world as well. Co-workers respect people who admit their own mistakes.
- **Strive For Excellence:** I started my career at 16 when I worked as a cashier in a grocery store. My parents told me then to do the best job I could for my employer and to try to learn as much as I could about doing the the job well. They're still telling me the same thing today — treat every job as a learning experience and measure your success in knowing you've performed your job as well as you can.
- **Be Courteous:** When I was young I remember visiting WBTV with Mother and noticed she was courteous to everyone, from the janitor to the president. She's never been so busy that she's ignored her calls, disregarded her correspondence or forgotten to compliment others on work well done.
- **Learn To Accept Criticism:** Mother has always gotten a huge amount of fan mail, and she reads almost every letter. Her TV show has thrived on suggestions from viewers. To me, the most difficult step is to accept criticism and to admit that someone else may have a better idea than mine.
- **Teach Other People:** Mother's career has been teaching people, and I think this is her greatest lesson. I can't think of any job in which an employee wouldn't be able to teach or help others. Mother has proved that the best lessons are indirect; the examples she has

shown and standards she has set are the best teaching I can remember.

P.S.: Although I've just quoted Mother's examples, my father is an equally great teacher. Much of Mother's success is directly attributable to the wisdom of my father. The public sees only half this team, but both help and teach other people.

November 28, 1977

Time Adds a Touch of Humor to Past

After new pains in my side, I was readmitted to Memorial, and I'm undergoing more cobalt treatments.

As I lie in my hospital bed, I think of the past. I remember some things I worried about when they happened but that look pretty amusing today.

For years, my TV show originated live, so anything that happened was seen immediately by the viewers. And there were some experiences I thought might take me off the air.

When our son John (he's now 21) was 4 or so, his father built him a little car from an old lawn mower. The motor would make it go all of 4 or 5 miles per hour.

With the straw hat he wore all the time, John looked so cute sitting in the car. We decided to take the car to the TV station so John could show how to drive it.

The WBTV building wasn't as large back then, and there was a grassy lawn just right for him to travel around. When the time came for the car feature, John drove the car around the grassy plot once. Then, he was to pick up his older sister, Betty Cole, and give her a once-around ride.

When she got on behind him, I noticed her skirt was in front of a wheel. I stepped forward to pick up the skirt so it wouldn't get caught. But John was ready to start. He did, and I was knocked down flat on the ground.

Time Adds a Touch of Humor to Past

I don't know exactly how I got up, but I did. In a ladylike way, I hope.

* * *

Our three children weren't on the show often, but if they did something special I thought others would enjoy, I'd invite them. When John was in kindergarten, he made a placemat using two pieces of wax paper with a leaf pressed in between. Thinking this would be helpful to kindergarten and Sunday school teachers, I invited John to show how he made this.

It was the day of the show. John did a beautiful job with the mat. I was so proud. My secretary was ready to usher him out after his appearance so I could finish the show.

Leading into my next commercial and trying to get him out of the studio, I offered John one of the frozen apple rolls I was getting ready to advertise.

He took one look at the plate and said, "I don't like those." I was horrified, and said quickly, "Yes, you do, John; you know you do." His reply was honest: "No, I don't."

Everyone in the studio and the control room just roared. I wanted to go through the floor. I knew we had lost a longtime sponsor.

But this surely proved we had viewers. Ladies would go into the supermarket and ask about the apple rolls Betty Feezor's boy did not like! Today, I still hear people ask which son wouldn't eat the apple rolls.

* * *

A couple of decades ago, after a lot of work and a considerable investment of money, my cookbook was published. I was so pleased.

I just knew when I announced the cookbook was ready, all my loyal viewers who had been writing for my free recipe sheets would order theirs immediately. I couldn't wait to get my mail. What happened? I had three orders!

I was sick! But today, "Carolina Recipes" Volume II is in the bookstores and in its third printing.

All these things prove the times that seem worst often turn out to be the funniest.

After watching the Carolinas Carrousel parade for so many years, I felt so honored that I was asked to be grand marshal. I was looking forward to Thanksgiving Day and the thrill of being part of this event. But I had to cancel and enjoy it on television.

I try not to dwell on the past, but remembering past events can help us be more optismistic about what's ahead.

Betty Feezor Grand Marshal of Carrousel

Betty Feezor, who has led thousands of television viewers to better homemaking for more than two decades, has a new leading role — grand marshal of the Carolinas Carrousel Parade Thanksgiving Day.

Parade officials announced her selection Saturday, saying she is "an important and sustaining personality in Charlotte, and she continues to spur new life and new energy to those who have a deep admiration for her."

December 5, 1977

From Hospital Bed

My Thanksgiving Day was spent in bed. I looked forward so much to participating in the Carrousel Parade but just couldn't make it. I did enjoy watching it on TV and almost needless to say, two of our children Betty Cole and Bob, enjoyed filling in for me.

My latest stay in Memorial, more than two weeks, has been longer than I expected. No one likes to be sick or likes to stay in the hospital, but it's good to have experienced and trained help to care for you. The friendly smiles and kind words from my nurses helped greatly.

Find Joy in Removing Routine from Your Daily Housekeeping

The prayers and encouraging words from so many of you mean so much. Thank you.

December 12, 1977

Find Joy in Removing Routine from Your Daily Housekeeping

After more than two weeks in the hospital, it is good to be home in quiet and familiar surroundings. There is no bed like your own.

Most of my time at home has been spent in bed . . . very little reading or watching TV, no energy to knit or write.

I remember once talking to a group of ladies about enjoying your work. Here are some of the things I said:

There are many joys in parenthood and homemaking — but life can get very "daily." Washing the same dishes every day, chasing the same dust and picking up and washing the same clothes ever week gets a little monotonous. Many years ago I learned a valuable lesson from one of the first TV newswomen: She said anything can become interesting if it is made newsworthy. And I think that works for common household tasks.

Instead of thinking of your washing as a chore, think of yourself as a textile chemist deciding on whether to use hot, warm or cold water. You also have the executive privilege of deciding on the type of detergent, water softener, bleach. etc. This turns the whole chore around.

Bob came in one day with the dirtiest shirt I had ever seen. When I asked him why he had gotten his shirt so dirty, he replied, "I know you like to get out spots and stains, Mom, so I thought I would make you happy this afternoon."

Or take sewing. Instead of thinking of yourself as just a seamstress, think of yourself as a designer. When you create a dress, it will be an original: No one will make the same mistakes on hers that you have made on yours!

If you hate to cook, think of yourself as a great chef. Learn to prepare one special meal you can depend on. Even if you have the same people for dinner often and even though you feed them the same thing, they will look forward to it just as you look forward to the specialty at a favorite restaurant.

You can use the same news technique to think of yourself as a safe and concerned chauffeur instead of just taking your turn at car pooling. When you are working in the yard, become a landscape artist. Even taking the garbage out can become more challenging if you think of yourself as sanitary engineer keeping your kitchen and family free from germs.

Dishwashing is one of the most dreaded homemaking jobs. As you clean up after a meal, see how many steps you can save as you clear the table and stack dishes or load the dishwasher. You can become an efficiency consultant.

These techniques for making life less "daily" could change your ideas about the drudgery of homemaking. For me, it works on everything except cleaning house, especially running the vacuum cleaner. I still haven't found a way to make that fun!

But for me today, it would be just great to be able to do any of these things — even run the vacuum cleaner.

December 19, 1977

I Have Heard God Speak, and That's Why I Believe

As the time comes for another chapter in my Observer diary, I find myself back in the hospital. I hope I won't be here too long.

I'm still not up too much — just a little reading and watching TV.

When Alan Newcomb, a reporter for WBTV for many years, died unexpectedly about a decade ago, he not only left complete and up-to-date scrapbooks, but also a written-out philosophy of life. It made me realize I didn't even have my thoughts in an orderly form in my head, much less on paper.

So I sat down and wrote out what I believe in:

There is a God. I have talked with Him, hearing Him tell me, "Yes," and "No" too many times for me not to believe, I am a child of God. He cares for me.

God has given me a very special blend of talent — perhaps not so great as those of other people, but my own special blend. He expects me to meake the most of these talents in developing them to their greatest potential.

God expects me to make the most of my circumstances. I must learn to accept my handicaps and learn to live with my mistakes — not complaining but increasing my depth of character by the way I handle these hardships.

God expects me to have a proper perspective in my life — putting God and his kingdom first, my family second, and my career or job or hobbies third.

God expects me to live one day at a time, so that at the end of that day I may feel that I have not wasted the precious few minutes I have on this earth, but that I have made some small contribution. I must not waste time and energy by grieving about the past nor worring about the future.

* * *

If I can live up to these goals each day, when my time comes to pass on, I will feel that God will be pleased with my efforts here on earth, and that I'll have made some lasting contribution.

December 26, 1977

Caring About Others Carries Its Own Rewards

This has been my second Christmas spent in the hospital. And I saw another birthday from here: My son Bob (he's 18 now) was born Dec. 23.

Caring About Others Carries Its Own Rewards

While I'm receiving more cobalt treatments, I'm spending a good deal of time reading my mail.

And I'm looking over some writing I did a few weeks ago. I wrote that the greatest rewards seemed to come through contributing to this world as we pass through.

As you think about your talents and opportunities, you may think you're much more limited than you really are. As you compare your capabilities with those you admire most, you may feel you've been left out as far as making your contribution.

Speak Kindly

But even if you can't write a great poem, you can speak kind words to those who need them. Just speaking to someone in a kind way can lift their spirits.

Perhaps you can't paint a picture, but a happy smile on your face can be the very picture that someone less fortunate is looking for.

Teach someone something. This is one of the greatest pleasures for us and for those we teach. These don't have to be monumental lessons.

Don't litter. Be careful how you use our forms of energy. Don't drive too fast. Don't pass on a critical statement about someone. I remember a cab driver in Honolulu who one Sunday drove some of us around trying to find an open restaurant. Finally, he took us to a quaint restaurant with a very large fish pond and the largest goldfish I ever saw. He seemed so interested in each one of us and in helping us find just what we needed that day.

Be Diligent

Then, in Holland, there was the baggage man who searched diligently in the rain for the "lost" half of our tour group of 44 people. He repeatedly returned to the front of the terminal searching for the bus with the other passengers and their luggage.

Both these people cared.

Recently I heard of a factory worker who was loved by so many because at lunchtime he was willing to listen, with attentive ears and heart, to the problems of his fellow workers. Many people are hungry for someone just to listen. What a simple way to make a contribution.

When I end this life, I would like it to be said of me:

"She lived in such a way that now that she isn't here, it matters that she was here."

<u>January 9, 1978</u>

Back Home

I am home from another hospital visit, and needless to say, I am very happy to be back home. Turner and the children had left the Christmas decorations and tree up, waiting for me. What a pleasure!

* * *

I'm putting all my energies right now into the things we are doing to get me better. I will not be doing any writing for a while as a result my column will be missing for a bit. I'll be doing a lot of just reading and resting.

* * *

The doctors could do nothing for Betty in the hospital. It was her request to return to her home.

She was confined to her bed but continued to read and watch TV. February 17th, her 53rd birthday, was very exciting for her. She was showered with cards and flowers. Her friends at WBTV sang "Happy Birthday" to her on the "Top of the Day Show."

On February 28 Betty died quietly at her home.

Funeral Meditation for Betty Feezor
by HARLEY DICKSON
March 1, 1978

Two selections from the New Testament — from Romans and the Gospel of John — are commonly used on occasions such as this. Several of their words and phrases seem to speak to me about the life and the faith of Betty Feezor, and to the special needs of her family and others of us gathered here today to honor her life.

"Let not your heart be troubled."
"I go to prepare a place for you. And if I go and prepare a place for you, I will come again, and receive you unto myself; that where I am, there ye may be also."
"The Father shall give you another Comforter, that he may abide with you for ever; even the Spirit of Truth; I will not leave you comfortless: I will come to you."

"As many as are led by the Spirit of God, they are the sons of God. The spirit itself beareth witness with our spirit, that we are the children of God: And if children, then heirs; heirs of God, and joint heirs with Christ."
"For I reckon that the suffering of this present time are not worthy to be compared with the glory which shall be revealed in us."
"And we know that in everything God works for good to them that love Him, to them who are called according to his purpose."

FAITH is a word that well describes the life of Betty Feezor. Hers was a real, radiant, genuine faith and it permeated all of her life. Her belief in the goodness and greatness of God was the source of her strength, the background of every action relating to family or friends, church or profession. She was specifically and unashamedly a Christian lady.

This service is our unique opportunity to celebrate her life and to affirm her faith in a setting of worship.

A motto which hung in Betty's kitchen reads, "Live so that when you are gone it will have mattered." This must have been important to her. She used those words to close the last devotional she prepared for her church circle, but was unable to give. She used similar words at the close of her last article in the Charlotte Observer on December 26th. "When I end this life, I would like it said of me, 'She lived in such a way that now she isn't here, it matters that she was here.' "

BETTY FEEZOR, YOU DID MATTER: YOU MATTERED FIRST AND MOST IMPORTANTLY TO YOUR FAMILY.

Her life and faith, intermingled with yours, made you a very unique and special family. And my prayer is that the guiding hand of God that led Betty and you for the past 25 years, will be with you in a very special way during these days when you feel so keenly this grief, this feeling of separation from one so important to you.

Betty did matter to her family and her influence and her faith will continue to matter.

BETTY FEEZOR, YOU MATTERED TO YOUR CHURCH.

She was active in all phases of its life, regularly present at its worship, but in a very special way she led what we affectionately call the "Betty Feezor Class" (though she never referred to it that way.)

The lectern from which she spoke is used by others now, but a beautiful piece of needlepoint, done by Betty during the past year, is a graphic reminder of her presence in the Christian Home Class, which she taught nearly every Sunday for over 5 consecutive years. The Bible says, "The Spirit bears witness with our spirit that we are the children of God," and Betty Feezor helped hundreds of persons at Providence Church across the years know that they too were children of God.

BETTY FEEZOR, YOU DID MATTER. AND YOU MATTERED TOO TO YOUR PROFESSIONAL ASSOCIATES AT WBT.

Many of you, like members of Betty's Christian Home Class, are here in this Sanctury in the special place reserved for honorary pallbearers. Everyone I know at WBTV always seemed to take special pride in being associated with Betty. And Betty loved all those with whom she worked, without any regard for position, sex, color, age or creed. To her, announcers, executives, cameramen, floor crew, technicians, clerical assistants, all were important people. She wouldn't settle for anything less than excellence

Funeral Meditation for Betty Feezor

and this spirit pulled out the best in those who worked with her.

AND, BETTY, YOUR LIFE AND FAITH MATTERED TO A WIDE CIRCLE OF FRIENDS IN YOUR TELEVISION AUDIENCE.

This number will never be known, but they are uniquely a part of her family, for Betty was a very special part of thousands of homes across twenty three years of broadcastings. Letters and calls and questions by the thousands during the past year have been only a small indication of the genuine concern of members of this wider family.

And Betty shared her life and faith with you, too. You knew her as a real, genuine, warm television personality and no one of you had any doubt about her faith. She was a Christian and didn't mind saying so, although her Christian witness was more obvious by who she was than any words she used to describe it.

During the past year Betty shared her personal struggle against cancer with this wider family, especially through her writing. She opened up doors of hope to many who had hidden their own fears in the dark recesses of their mind.

Some would ask me occasionally — "I know what she said in the newspaper, but how does she really feel?" The truthful reply always was, "I know of nothing important about her feelings that she has not shared with all of you." And this sharing of her faith will certainly rank as one of her most important witnesses. Her courage and her faith have been an inspiration to us all. I look forward to the time, hopefully very soon, when her autobiography, written during the past year, will be published, and the story of her life and the inspiration of her courageous faith can be shared with an even wider family.

BETTY FEEZOR, TODAY WE AFFIRM WITH YOU OUR FAITH IN THE GOODNESS AND THE GREATNESS OF GOD. WE SHARE THE HOPE THAT "THE SUFFERINGS OF THIS PRESENT TIME ARE NOT WORTHY TO BE COMPARED TO THE GLORY THAT SHALL BE REVEALED IN YOU" AS YOU NOW ENTER THE JOYOUS REWARDS OF EVERLASTING LIFE.

And together we affirm, "YOU REALLY DID MATTER --- AND YOU STILL DO."

PRAYER -
    Gracious God, how great Thou art —
— For giving us Betty Feezor, whose life has been lived among us in such a special way.
    How great Thou art —
— For giving us a faith that such a life as this will truly never end.
And —
    How great Thou art — for giving us the comforting presence of your Spirit, which now surrounds this family and all those who share their loss.
    How great Thou art — for giving each of us the opportunity to live a life of usefulness, in a way that will matter.

And now —
    May the Lord bless you and keep each of you, may the Lord make his face to shine upon you and be gracious unto you. The Lord lift up His countenance upon you and give you peace. Amen.

PART III

TRIBUTES TO BETTY

As Death Came, She Was Ready

by David Lawrence Jr.
Editor, *The Observer*

I am not saddened by Betty Feezor's death. Betty would not want that.

A blessing, I thought when I heard the news. A blessing because there would be no more pain for Betty Feezor. A blessing because she will go to the place she always wanted to go, a place she always saw as her destination.

God, I know, must be pleased today. One of His best friends is with Him.

When I think of the word "Christian" as I believe it's best used, I think of two people. One of them, Betty Feezor, died yesterday; the other is Kays Gary, who writes a column for The Observer.

I was in another city yesterday morning when I was awakened by a telephone call telling me Betty had died. Through the day, I thought of what to write because I wanted everyone to know how much she meant to me and to so many other people.

Late in the afternoon I was in a plane approaching Charlotte, coming home. We circled, without explanation, for at least 15 minutes. Our pilot finally announced in his best it's-important-to-be-calm voice that there was a problem with the hydraulic brake lines and, maybe, the nose gear wouldn't work. (Everything would be fine, he said, but it's "better to be safe than sorry.") I was not reassured.

As we came in for a landing some while later, we could see a half-dozen emergency vehicles with red lights flashing. We touched down — all was right — amid the cheers and the handclapping from nervous and fortunate people who felt relief and joy.

In those minutes before landing, I thought about life and death. Mine. And Betty Feezor's. I thought how Betty Feezor was ready for death; in fact looked forward to it. She had completed her work in this world.

How many of us will be able to say the same at our moment of death?

* * *

I knew Betty Feezor only as a name, a celebrity, until about a year ago, when it was announced she had brain and lung cancer. We first met over a pot of vegetable soup in her kitchen. I had suggested, timidly and awkwardly, that perhaps she could help others with a weekly diary of her experiences in battling cancer. She *knew* instantly that in those diaries she could continue giving of herself.

Through almost a year of those tape-recorded diaries, until she could do them no more, she spoke of her struggle and her faith. People came to me — and wrote her — to say how much her diaries meant to them. In all that time, Betty never lost, despite pain at times that must have been enormous, her faith in God.

A person confident of her abilities on camera, she did worry whether she could write. Of course she, of great talent, could.

* * *

I last saw her little more than a week ago on her 53rd birthday. She was home, in her bedroom, when my secretary, Dottie Adams, and I brought in the cake. Betty smiled, said a few words, but she obviously was terribly weak.

We told her we loved her and left her room. We went into Betty's kitchen, and her husband, Turner, said softly and with tears, "I think she realizes now that she's not going to make it. But she hasn't lost her spirit."

The person I most worry about now is Turner Feezor. Betty's where she will be happy and without pain. Their three children are almost grown, and Betty and Turner raised them right. They're going to be fine.

Turner will miss, at least for now, his great love, Betty.

Turner Feezor's past year of torment, of course, has been a time when he could not turn to the person he always turned to for solace and hope. But he seemed at peace when I talked to him last night, He told me that children John and Bob were home when their mother died, and that daughter Betty Cole had arrived home later in the day.

As Death Came, She Was Ready

Turner spoke of Betty Feezor's last few days, mostly ones of "resting and sleeping, and thankfully not a lot of pain." He was happy Betty could die at home, with the people she loved, and not at a hospital. "She died as peaceful as anybody could go," he said.

Turner needs our love and prayers.

Like Turner, we will all miss Betty, who did so much for us.

Betty Was A Lady

BY CHARLES H. CRUTCHFIELD

It was my privilege to serve as President of the Jefferson-Pilot Broadcasting Company during the twenty-two years when Betty Feezor was reigning — unchallenged — as the Number One homemaking television personality in the nation.

We knew, shortly after Betty came with WBTV, that she was an individual of rare skill — a legitimate authority on cooking, sewing, and all aspects of homemaking, What we perhaps didn't realize at the time was that she was a remarkable human being — a person who, through the strength of her personality and character, could inspire unparalleled loyalty and affection.

But it didn't take long for us to see what a jewel Betty really was. The usual months and months of "building" an audience which most new television personalities require simply weren't necessary with her. Betty "caught on" with viewers at the very beginning. She was an immediate "hit".

As one who had studied — since 1929 — that difficult to define quality that some people have to attract legions of followers, I tried to determine what it was that endeared people to her and kept them loyal for more than a generation. I finally concluded that — over and above her talents, which were enormous — her secret of success was her sincerity. She was herself completely. She was cut from whole cloth. People instinctively realized this, and responded.

If there is one word that sums her up best, it is *"lady"*. Betty was a lady — in every sense of the word. And, it is too much to hope that we will ever see her equal again.

Betty Feezor: Charlotte's Favorite Dish

by MICHELLE FRANK

TV Mirror, April 1970

Betty Feezor runs into problems that are unlikely to happen to a typical housewife. If she isn't being run over by her young son with a go-cart made from a lawnmower or having her electric blender drop to the floor and cut her leg in front of thousands of people, then to her the day isn't active. It's difficult being a housewife all right, but Betty holds a few other titles. Among them, economics consultant to the homemakers of North Carolina and South Carolina, Tennessee and Virginia. All the other women are with her from day to day as Betty stars on WBTV's "Betty Feezor Show" weekdays from 1 to 1:30 P.M. in Charlotte, N.C. That's a lot of cooking, sewing, decorating, gardening and child advice she has handed out in the seventeen years she's been on the air. "I've had three leaves of absence for three children," she adds. That's dedication!

"What I love about the show is that it is timely and very much down to earth so that it may answer a viewer's need that very day. Also, it seems to communicate well with the men; they make up about ten percent of the audience," she says.

Betty doesn't restrict her guest lineup to the field of homemaking, instead, they cover a wide range of areas, from politics including Mrs. Rose Kennedy, Mrs. Richard Nixon, to the entertainment industry with E.G. Marshall and the world of beauty with Anita Colby. "Once Mrs. Luther Hodges, wife of the governor of North Carolina was to be my guest. She didn't arrive until five ,minutes after air time, so I met her for the first time along with my viewers on the air," she reminisces. "And when Anita Colby was to be my guest, I was very nervous since she is so beautiful. She was very lovely and gracious and didn't make me feel as awkward standing beside her as I had feared."

Her audience, made up of young homemakers, has been spurred into entering contests and Betty boasts of having received over

12,000 letters. "I was thrilled at the sight of it even though it did crowd up on my desk."

A dedicated chef, she prefers the joy of teaching women how to sew. "There are recipes and directions for food everywhere, but many of the sewing and tailoring tricks are not printed. When a woman writes me that as a result of watching my show she has bought a machine and started making clothes for her family, this is real satisfaction," Betty admits.

And the show just fell into her lap. "I moved as a young bride to Charlotte, and being a home economist with a desire to help homemakers I felt that God has this to me as my mission field — to be able to go into homes that many other women would never be able to enter, with teaching in mind. it is not a job to me, but a very pleasant experience and a very special opportunity to teach."

And because of her enthusiasm, she is the recipient of the Homemaker of the Year Award, Woman of the Year in Foods, and many other delicious-sounding honors. Betty has earned them, having a bachelor of science degree in home economics from the University of Tennessee.

Born with a spoon, needle and thread clenched in her little fist on February 17, 1925, in Texarkana, Texas, Betty always liked to sew and had learned to do handwork at the age of 8. Being an only child, she admits she had more time alone to develop her homemaking hobbies. "We moved to Fayetteville, Arkansas and then to Little Rock where I finished high school and decided to head for home economics as my major in college. My reasons for this was that I liked it and felt that it would be a good field for women." It was also easier to catch a husband!

From then on, her career was as smooth as apple pie. It was while she was a home demonstration agent on tv in Greensboro that her reputation followed wherever she went. "When I moved to Charlotte from Greensboro, the manager of the station wrote WBTV and suggested that they look me up if they needed someone in my field. They did. I filled in for the lady then doing a cooking show for two weeks, and eventually I was offered my own show."

She was a natural for televsion, but she had a difficult time getting adjusted to the mechanics. "I had a hard time learning to read the teleprompter copy and had a hard time stopping talking when told."

Betty Feezor: Charlotte's Favorite Dish

But those were to be followed by several amusing accidents like whole gelatin salads landing, not on the plate but in her lap!

There's no doubt that she is a success. her show was rated second in the US among other wopmen's interest programs and is currently being shown over WWBT in Richmond, Va. Since thousands of women see her, when does her family see her?

"Probably my biggest hobby is my family. With two teenagers and a 9 year old son I don't have that much time. When I do, we pack up the family and go from the seashore to the mountains, just traveling around." But with a completely free day, she'll go downtown and shop without having to look at a clock or take along a list of things to buy for her show.

Her husband, Turner Cole, is well taken care of because he is the first one who tests her on recipes. The two met while they were working together as home demonstration agents in North Carolina. And next to Turner, the joys of her life are Betty, John and Robert, the Feezor's three children. "My daughter loves to cook but she won't major in home economics. She'd rather take up math," the lady of the house says.

The Feezor's live in a new home with two kitchens of course. "That's because we all like to cook," she adds. Their home is complete with 18 years' worth accumulation of furniture, which is comfortable with lots of living in evidence, according to Betty.

Aside from being fond of her domestic chores, she has joined the publishing world as the author of two published cookbooks, with a third on the way. With all of her elaborate cooking, she still contends that chocolate cake is her favorite dish. And Betty is Charlotte's favorite dish.

A Lost Warmth — It Matters to Thousands Betty Feezor Was Here

BY LEW POWELL AND KEN ALLEN

Betty Feezor, whose impact on people's lives spread beyond the television home economics show she hosted for 23 years, will be buried today in Charlotte's Evergreen Cemetery on Central Avenue.

She died of cancer at 6 A.M. Tuesday at her home. She was 53.

The warmth she projected through her private life, making her a favorite in the south Charlotte neighborhood where she lived and in the Providence United Methodist Church where she worshiped and taught Sunday school for 15 years.

In the last 11 months, she reached a new audience as she wrote about her battle with cancer in a column, "Betty Feezor's Diary," for The Observer.

WBTV will broadcast her funeral service live at 2 P.M. today from Providence United Methodist Church. The family asks that, instead of flowers, people donate to the Betty Feezor Scholarship Fund in care WBTV, 1 Julian Price Place, Charlotte 28208.

WBTV broadcast a 30-minute special Tuesday night, "Betty Feezor: What A Difference You Made in Our Lives."

From 1956, when her show went from two days a week to five, until her retirement in February 1977, Mrs. Feezor held the top spot in Charlotte daytime television.

About 100,000 households across the Piedmont — two-thirds of all sets in use between 1 and 1:30 P.M. weekdays — tuned in for her live cooking and sewing tips. The show was taped and shown on WBTV's sister station, WWBT in Richmond.

"I'm not a gourmet cook," she once said. "Julia Child is a success at night, but she wouldn't go over with my audience."

Charles Crutchfield, president of Jefferson Pilot Broadcasting

A Lost Warmth — It Matters to Thousands Betty Feezor Was Here

Co. throughout Mrs. Feezor's tenure with the company-owned WBTV, said her show has been hard to replace.

"When Betty Feezor became ill, we replaced her program with 'Top of The Day.' " Crutchfield recalled Tuesday. "But it took a dozen or more people to fill that slot. She did it all herself.

"But with this new show ... we're still having a hard time gathering up all her sponsors."

Response to the Betty Feezor Show appeared not only in the ratings, but also in sales of her three cookbooks (more than 70,000 copies) and mail from viewers (about 5,000 requests a month for recipe sheets on such dishes as Hot Dog Fondue and Easy Freezy Lemon Pie.)

"I told my husband I would move anywhere his job took him," wrote one viewer, "as long as I could still watch Betty Feezor."

Said another: "You have become as one of my family, and if I have to miss you on any day, it's as if I have missed one of my own children."

She especially enjoyed letters from young homemakers who remembered hating the show as children — "My mother watched it when I didn't want to" — but grew to appreciate it.

Piedmont home economists became used to hearing audience members interject, "But that's not the way Betty Feezor does it. . . ."

Carolyn Leonard, home economist with the Mecklenburg County Agricultural Extension Service, said Mrs. Feezor's popularity made the work of home extension agents easier.

"She loved home economics," Mrs. Leonard said. "She had a keen sense of doing things that were professional and ethical.

"She could reach thousands (through television) that we couldn't reach in a live audience. Her philosophy was that every day there was someone out there whose life she could make better. . . ."

She and Turner Feezor, a farm equipment salesman, married in 1952 and soon moved to Charlotte. Within a year WBTV offered her part-time cooking and sewing assignments, and she was on her way to becoming, in the truest sense, a household word across the Piedmont.

Last year on her 52nd birthday, her doctor discovered she had cancer of the brain and the lung — cancers that were treated with radiation and chemotherapy.

Although she did little television work after her illness, she remained busy. Her weekly columns on her struggle with cancer began appearing in The Observer.

In introducing Betty Feezor's Diary, Observer Editor David Lawrence Jr. wrote:

"Betty Feezor isn't scared to talk about cancer. In fact, she thinks we'd all be better off if we talked about it a lot more. . . . She hopes that diary, which she'll dictate into a tape recorder, will help you understand what it's like to have cancer and how important faith is in fighting it."

Lawrence said Tuesday his year-long association with her had convinced him of her faith and courage. "She has this remarkable sort of faith, in God and in human beings."

Dottie Adams, Lawrence's secretary, grew close to Mrs. Feezor over the months as she would go to the Feezor home at 6217 Glenridge Rd. in the Olde Stonehaven section to pick up the columns.

"I'm not a very religious person. But hers was so obvious that it had an impact on me and the way I look at things."

When her illness was known, the community tried to return some of the warmth Mrs. Feezor had given over the years.

The N.C. Home Economics Association created a scholarship in her name. She was chosen Grand Marshal of last Thanksgiving's Carolinas Carrousel parade, but was in a hospital on parade day. Daughter Betty Cole Feezor, a Chapel Hill mathematician, and son Bob, a senior at East Mecklenburg High School, filled in for her.

She concluded her last column, published Dec. 26, with an epitaph: "When I end this life, I would like it to be said of me: 'She lived in such a way that now that she isn't here, it matters that she was here.' "

March 1, 1978

Betty: Neighbor to Thousands
by ALLEN NORWOOD
Charlotte News

Most everybody who has turned on a television set at midday in Piedmont North Carolina during the past couple of decades has a treasured Betty Feezor story. One of ours is about the mother from a large, northern city who came south for the first time to visit her daughter in Charlotte.

"Let's go, mother," said the daughter. "Let me show you the sights and treat you to a meal at my favorite restaurant."

"Not now," said the mother. "I'm watching Betty."

The mother had discovered on her first day here what two-thirds of the Piedmont's viewers already knew: The place to be during her half-hour every day was with Betty Feezor. Such was the attraction of her homemaking show, which endured for 24 years on WBTV. And she was immediately and always "Betty," just as if she were a neighbor.

Then there was the elementary school student from Huntersville who wanted to do something for Betty Feezor after she had become ill. The teacher, unsure of how to handle the request, asked for a show of hands from those who knew who Betty Feezor was. Every little hand went up. The youngsters colored get-well cards and carefully printed their best wishes.

Betty Feezor died yesterday after a long and valiant fight against cancer. She is survived by her husband, Turner C. Feezor, and three children. She will be sorely missed by those who worked with her over the years at WBTV. A scholarship fund will honor her memory. But there is more.

Even as she hosted the most popular daytime television show in this area, Betty Feezor maintained that her career was not the most important part of her life. Home and family came first. What she managed to do — through warmth, skill and hard work — was share her home and welcome hundreds of thousands of viewers into her television family.

Those who visited with her, learned from her and suffered with her won't remember Betty as a television personality, but as a friend. And that's quite a legacy.

Twentieth Anniversary

by W.J.JORGENSON

This is going to be more of a love letter than an interoffice memo. That's because it's about the fact that on Friday, April 30, you will be celebrating your twentieth anniversary with the company.

And what a remarkable twenty years they are I've been in the television business since it began and nowhere in the industry do I know of a record like the one you have established with WBTV.

When you signed on with us in 1956, cooking shows were regular daytime program fare on about every TV station. But in a few years only the good ones were still there. You broadened the content of your show and innovated, and it continued to grow while the few remaining fell.

Today, the "Betty Feezor Show" is completely unique. It is not only the sole survivor among shows of its kind, it is one of the most dominant local shows in the country. The competition has thrown everything in the book at you including most recently "Mary Hartman, Mary Hartman" in an effort to dislodge you. Some stations have had remarkable success with Norman Lear's seamy soap opera in knocking off such formidable competition as prime evening news strips. That's undoubtedly why WSOC decided to throw it against you. Once again they have failed because long before now the "Betty Feezor Show" was an impregnable institution.

Betty, I don't want to get lyrical about this but what you have accomplished in those twenty years is so exceptional I just can't be modest about it. No doubt about it, you and Clyde and Doug have played major roles in making WBTV what it is today. But *your* contribution is the most unique of all.

What can I possibly say to you on your twentieth anniversary, that could ever express the admiration I have for you and the gratitude I feel for the day you decided to join us? There just aren't words.

Forgive me, but like I said at the beginning — this is more of a love letter.

Happy Anniversary, Betty!

I'm looking forward to your twenty-fifth.

Tribute to Betty

From my teen-age years, Betty was my friend
A daily visit she paid
She taught me how to bake a cake;
She showed me how to hang a shade.

The pillows in my den say "Betty,"
The cookies in the jar.
A dress that in my closet hangs;
with her help I did come so far.

I always felt she was my neighbor;
A close and devoted pal,
Good wife and mother, a true Christian Lady,
But still an "all right" "O.K." gal.

Now my heart is so heavy,
My head in sorrow is bowed.
Betty is gone. I'll see her face no more.
I cry my grief aloud.

But wait! I tell myself in my sorrow—
Look up and see the good!
The clay is gone, 'tis true—
The spirit still shines strong, like the "Betty Lamp"—

She still lives; in her family; and with God.
Betty's deep faith, this past year, led so many,
She shared her troubles with all who grieved.
She fought "the good fight" to the finish.
She never hid and cried "why me?"

She was strong, and she was brave.
She was a fighter; who finally went down.

But I know; she was lifted up again.
She wears many bright stars in her crown.

I think God touched Betty Feezor.
I think God looked down from his throne—
Her suffering here was ended;
Her mission here was finished;
When God said:
> "I want you with me now, Betty"
> "Betty, come back home."

Jo Nell Mason

I HAVE A NOMINATION FOR THE
"TELEVISION HALL OF FAME—"
  EVERY HOUSEWIFE WILL AGREE, WHEN,
I DISCLOSE HER NAME—
  SHE HAS VISITED ALL OUR KITCHENS
HELPING GET THE MEALS ON TIME—
  AND ENRICHED THE LIVES OF THOUSANDS,
JUST AS SHE HAS ENRICHED MINE —
  SHE GAVE US WORDS OF WISDOM —TO
LIVE BY FROM DAY TO DAY —
  SHE CHASED AWAY THE SHADOWS, WHEN
THE WORLD SEEMED DARK AND GRAY —
  RECIPES FOR BODY HUNGER — RECIPES FOR
HUNGRY SOULS —
  MAKING EVERYBODY HAPPY — SEEMS TO BE
HER HUMBLE GOAL —
  THE BETSY ROSS'ES — JOANS OF ARC AND
ALL THE MOLLY PITCHERS
  HAS EVER REACHED SO MANY FOLKS —
OR MADE MORE HOMES MORE RICHER —
  SHE MAY NOT OWN AN "EMMY" — OR AN
"OSCAR" OR "NOBEL PRIZE" —
  BUT WHEN "NICE AND "WONDERFUL CAME"
AROUND — THEY GAVE HER A GENEROUS SLICE —
  I SEARCHED AND SEARCHED BUT COULD NOT
FIND AN OLD CARD OR A NEW —
  TO SAY THE THINGS THAT'S IN MY HEART
THAT ONLY I CAN DO —
  MUCH LOVE AND PRAYERS AND GOOD WISHES —
FOLLOWS HER WHERE - 'ERE SHE GOES —
  GOD WILLING SHE'LL COME BACK TO US —
ON *"THE BETTY FEEZOR SHOW"*

  God Bless
  Eleanor Owings

TRIBUTES TO BETTY

A Memorial to Betty Feezor

by Evelyn Carter

When we heard of Betty's illness
    We were distressed so much
Cause we knew in our own minds
    Her pots and pans no more she'd touch.

Every day we waited for the clock to turn to one
    And she would come on smiling
Bright as the morning sun.

It seemed when she was sewing
    The things just fell in place
    And she was oh so confident
    And did it with such grace.

I sent for all her recipes
    Not one did I ever fail
    And she used the ones I sent to her
    By telephone or mail.

The Kiwanians had her several times
    To talk for our spring event
And the "Y" was overflowing
    With county clubs — their time well spent.

When on February 28 we heard the news
    That Betty had just died
I knew her suffering was over
    But I sat quietly down and cried.

I know that she is happy
    And that in Heaven if there is any cooking done
She has the job of fixing
    Cookies for the little ones.

A Memorial to Betty Feezor

From the Book of Second Timothy
   Something that fits her right.
It's such a beautiful passage
   When it says "I've fought a good fight."

I am now ready to be offered
   That great faith I have kept
My course I have finished
   Not once have I wept.

   Henceforth there is laid up for me
   In Heaven a crown whom the Lord, the righteous
   judge will give me
And on my countenance not a frown.

Betty Feezor Fans Set up Scholarship
by Kays Gary

Betty Feezor fans, frustrated for lack of a way to express their admiration for their homemaking guru, need fret no longer.

Home economics professionals, many inspired to their careers by the woman who for 25 years has magnetized armies of housewives with her WBTV noonday show, on Tuesday announced a Betty Feezor Scholarship Fund to enable others to pursue the homemaking art.

WBTV kicked it off with a contribution of $1,000, The Charlotte Observer followed with $500 and Hugh Ashcraft, president Harris-Teeter Supermarkets, rose to offer another$1,000.

It was immediately clear that if every Feezor follower mails a contribution to The Betty Feezor Scholarship Fund, c/o WBTV, Charlotte, N.C., 28208, the homemaking art, a la Feezor, is insured in the area for generations.

The announcement came at a luncheon on WBTV's outdoor Pine Terrace, cohosted by the southwestern region of the N.C. Home Economics Association. The sunny day with birds flitting through the nearby pines, was perfect except. . . .

Betty wasn't there. An attack of flu and doctors' orders had kept her home to conserve her strength in her battle with cancer.

She watched the televised affair, though, declared herself thrilled and "so grateful to think a girl could further her education in home economics with a scholarship bearing my name."

Betty's 17-year-old son, Bob, accepted the association's symbolic silver lamp inscribed, "To One of The Greatest — Betty Feezor."

"Mother is going to treasure this for a long time to come," he said.

Bobbie Ross, chairperson of the association's 18-county southwestern region, Harriette McDowell Holton of Shelby, Eleanor McIntyre of Charleston, Carolyn Leonard of the N.C. Extension Service and others spoke of their commitments inspired early-on by Betty.

Betty Feezor Fans Set Up Scholarship

Said Ms. Ross: "No one knows her impact better than other Piedmont home economists, who have become used to seeing a hand go up in the audience followed by a reproving voice saying, 'But that's not the way Betty Feezor does it!'"

The scholarship, for aspiring home economics majors living in North Carolina or South Carolina, will be awarded annually on the basis of merit and need. The selection committee includes members of Carolinas colleges offering home economics majors, plus state and industrial home economists.

The whole deal is beautiful.

And awesome.

But so, by any measure — metric, heaven or Earth — so is Betty, the gal I once affectionately called "motor mouth." This Betty Feezor Scholarship recipe is a winner.

Forget the shortening and go heavy on the icing.

No matter that it's tax deductible.

It's an ever-lovin' bonus where it counts most as Betty has always known.

At home.

To the TIMES—NEWS

I have just heard over radio that my friend, Betty Feezor, WBTV, Charlotte, succumbed to a year's battle with cancer. Betty has meant more to housewives and TV viewers in this area than any other personality I know of — giving us insight, hope, delight and ingenuity in the planning and execution of good meals, good grooming and decorating.

But the heart of Betty Feezor was a Christian faith that was so beautiful that she always unconsciously shared with her friends and viewers.

She was a Sunday School teacher, a great mother and such a good daughter! She often spoke of her mother and the wonderful help she was in preparing her TV programs.

One of my happiest memories is having a meal in her modest and lovely home In Charlotte when she entertained the North Carolina Chapter of American Women in Radio and Television.

She was a "Star" and we will continue to miss her. How appropriate that her memorial will be a Betty Feezor Scholarship.

I trust she left a heritage that will not leave the American scene.

Her friend,
Jo Kuykendall

Hers Was a Friendly Voice

BY W.STANLEY MOORE, EDITOR
The News Herald, Morganton, N. C.

Charlotte's WBTV (Channel 3) is the oldest television facility in this region and it has functioned from the earliest days of the industry. In fact, Channel 3 has grown up with it and so have some of its staff members.

One of the best known of the TV personalities in these parts is Betty Feezor, the specialist in homemaking — presenting a special half-hour program five days a week to bring household hints, recipes, sewing tips, and general miscellany.

For 23 years Mrs. Feezor (this is her formal name, never used by her TV audience who referred to her simply as Betty or Betty Feezor.

A woman of charm and grace who was never at a loss for words, she projected an image altogether wholesome and helpful.

The editor of The News Herald, who wouldn't know a recipe from a dress pattern, became a fan in the strangest sort of way. A few years ago while whiling away a second prolonged period in a hospital — this one a mere 48 days when hepatitis following a more hectic illness robbed him of energy, appetite and almost everything else — he had the benefit of a television set in his room. There was little he found to interest him in the daytime tube offering, but Betty Feezor became his favorite. This wasn't because he knew what she was talking about. He knew that she knew what she was talking about, and he found her voice was soothingly friendly. The theme music of the Betty Feezor show ushered in a pleasing half-hour period.

Betty Feezor was the dame with the friendly voice and he liked the voice and he liked her. He never got to tell her about the therapeutic effect of her program.

Dear God: Re Betty Feezor

Charlotte Observer, March 2, 1978

MEMORANDUM
To: God
From Betsy Seymour
Concerning: A letter of introduction for Mrs. Betty Feezor

Your Son told us that in your house are many rooms. I sure hope one is a BIG kitchen. A dear friend of ours is coming your way and a few facts would help you in proper placement of this angel.

Your TV viewing time may be scarce, so please allow me to fill you in. Betty Feezor starred in a midday TV series in which she ministered to the needs of thousands of homemakers, both in the homemaking arts and in spiritual matters. A source of joy, cheer and information, her calm, delightful manner lifted many a low spirit and inspired all who met her, over the airways and off.

Please know that if the heavenly kitchen is in need of inspiration, a skilled leader is in your midst. Her smile will fill your hearts and her talents your tummies. In needle art she is very proficient. If a new robe you need, a masterpiece you'll receive.

But where she really excels is with people. If you have a down-in-the dumps angel, Betty's your girl. As a people-lover, an interpreter of other's gifts and talents and a spiritual counselor and teacher, she'll be a real helpmate.

Heaven sure is a lucky place. You've received a very special person who will make the Pearly Gates shine a little brighter. Please use her wonderful talents in a very special way because only You know what a "jewel of great price" she really is.

P.S. — Be patient with our tears, God, because even though we know she's extremely happy and without pain, we miss her so very much. Thank you for the 53 years we were given to love and enjoy her.

BETSY SEYMOUR

Concord